Child Employment in Britain

A Social and Psychological Analysis

Sandy Hobbs and Jim McKechnie

THE STATIONERY OFFICE: SCOTLAND

© The Stationery Office Limited 1997

The Stationery Office Limited
South Gyle Crescent
Edinburgh EH12 9EB

Applications for reproduction should be made to
The Stationery Office Limited

First published 1997

British Library Cataloguing in Publication Data
A catalogue record for this book is available from the British Library

ISBN 0 11 495816 5

Contents

Preface		vii
List of Tables and Figures		xi
Introduction		1
Chapter 1	**Child Employment: Some Issues**	5
Chapter 2	**The Extent of Child Employment in Britain**	24
Chapter 3	**The Nature of Children's Jobs**	39
Chapter 4	**A Closer Look at Cumbria**	62
Chapter 5	**Work and Education**	79
Chapter 6	**Costs and Benefits**	96
Chapter 7	**Some Conclusions**	116
Appendix 1	A Note on Sources	140
Appendix 2	Cases of Child Labour in British Newspapers	142
Appendix 3	Standard Grade Performance and Work Status	146
References		147
Index		152

Preface

This book enjoys the good fortune of appearing at precisely the right moment to contribute to a lively international debate about the nature of child work and its significance for the well-being and development of children who engage in it. This global discussion stems from growing conviction among child advocates, social science researchers, child labour experts and others that the conventional wisdom regarding the work of children, whether in rich countries or poor, is seriously out of step with current realities. It has become commonplace to note that many of the most popular assumptions about which children work, why they work, the nature of the work they do, and the impact of that work on themselves and society are poorly supported by credible research. As a matter of fact, when proper studies become available they often expose common beliefs to be mere myths. And, just as disconcertingly, their findings tend to underline the enormous diversity between cultures and situations. The relationships between work and the well-being of children are more complex than is popularly recognized, and we do not know very much about them, except perhaps in the extreme circumstances of work that is either especially dangerous or particularly educational.

These issues have in recent years become especially visible, for all countries, except the USA and Somalia, have now ratified the 1989 UN Convention on the Rights of the Child. This Convention obligates its member states to, above all, make 'the best interests of the child' a primary consideration in all policies that affect children. This means that governments need to be able to show that their child labour policies, for example, do in fact serve the best interests of the country's children. Under the terms of the Convention, this is normally understood to mean that such policies effectively protect children's well-being and promote their physical, mental and social development. This is an important issue because, in various countries, some children's advocates and working children themselves have insisted that current child labour policies are in fact inimical to their best interests. This throws into high relief the question of when work is good for children and should be permitted as an opportunity, and when it is harmful and should be prohibited or regulated. The state of our knowledge is not now adequate to make such fine discriminations.

Emerging perspectives on childhood and on child labour have shown our knowledge about child work and workers to be especially thin in at least three critical areas. First of all, our understanding of just who works, when and how much, and doing precisely what, is generally so incomplete that we frequently draw the wrong conclusions. In most countries, official data is so flawed that published statistics may be more misleading than helpful. It is no wonder that many policies and programmes affect primarily children in relatively harmless work while children who work in scandalously dangerous or exploitative conditions are left unprotected. For example, there is considerable evidence that young girls working as live-in maids may be in particular danger of physical, sexual and psychological abuse but they tend to be overlooked, even though they are in many countries among the most numerous of working children. We also need to understand more about the reasons why children work. While many discussions of child labour causes stress the imperatives of poverty and paint a grim picture of forced exploitation, field studies increasingly show that even under conditions of poverty many children work not only out of necessity, but also because they want to. They value learning, independence or other benefits they feel their work accords them. We need a more nuanced perspective on the problem.

From the high degree of concern expressed by many governments, trade unions and industry associations, United Nations agencies, child advocates and others, one could be excused for assuming that solid scientific findings undergird the claim that working generally undermines the well-being and development of at least young children. In fact, research of this type is extremely scarce, which is amazing when one considers that untold millions of children spend more of their week at work than at school. We do not know much about how the typical work experience of most children actually affects them for good or for ill, and it has been observed that this lack of empirical evidence calls into question the merit of many child labour policies in both rich and poor countries. Such studies as do exist have looked mostly at the physical health effects of certain types or conditions of work already known to be dangerous. We know next to nothing about the relationship between work and the psychological and social development of children; child development psychologists are only now starting to explore this issue. Research of this type is not easy, in part because it is necessary to develop tools that probe work-related questions within the framework of modern concepts of child development which depart from earlier standard models that posited childhood as a set of fixed stages that all children pass through on the way to an end point labelled 'maturity'. Newer social science stresses the importance of contextual factors, the internal resources children bring to their own development, and the variety of ways in which the two interact. It sees not one universal model of childhood, but many childhoods, and the role and effects of children's work certainly differ from one to the other.

We also know surprisingly little about what is effective in preventing or remediating work detrimental to children. This may come as a bit of a shock to the general public, which probably believes that the efficacy of child labour laws, workplace inspection, compulsory education and other traditional measures have long been demonstrated. Otherwise, one might think, these hoary mechanisms to control child labour would not have been around so long, in the case of Britain since about 1833. While few dispute that these conventional approaches have at least some effect over their long history, most who have looked into the matter recognize that other social, economic, political, technological and ideological forces have been much more influential in determining whether children work and the kinds of work they undertake. There is a gathering consensus that new thinking and practices must be introduced in order to deal effectively with these other factors according to their importance in each country. This seems especially true for the developing countries, where interventions first developed for an industrializing Europe in the 19th and early 20th centuries do not seem well suited for a radically different sort of context. Even in the rich countries of Europe and North America some are now suggesting that perhaps the whole matter of children's work – including what work is and is not appropriate for children – should be re-examined from the bottom up, and new methods for addressing it adopted as good sense indicates. This implies more diversity in policy; interventions designed to be effective in, say, India or Nigeria may not be applicable to Britain, and vice versa.

The upshot of all this is to foster a new appreciation for pluralism and cultural relativity in approaching child labour issues. It also emphasizes the need for in-depth field studies that raise and answer all the big questions for each society specifically. This implies that approaching the issue through international rules that apply uniformly to all societies might not be as beneficial for children as people now advocating global measures – such as prohibitions against imports made with the involvement of children – would hope. More carefully targeted responses are needed. It is increasingly recognized that public policy and other action to regulate or compensate for the work of children should be guided by rigorous empirical research, which, for each society, clearly defines problems where they exist, suggests lines of action that might be most appropriate, and monitors interventions to assess their effects on the children and families involved. But there is still considerable uncertainty about how to undertake such empirical research and link it to policy in a practical manner.

This book, which considers the case of Great Britain, presents by example a picture of what a carefully empirical consideration of the issues in a given country might look like, especially in countries where a body of research into child work issues already exists. It addresses many of the critical questions mentioned above, but with due caution that recognizes the limits of the data. It is eminently down-to-earth and practical while being academically rigorous enough to support intelligent policy debate in Britain. Rather than venturing to illumine problems and possibilities for the whole world in abstract, it focuses in a craftsmanly way on a particular place and a particular time. It approaches the all-important question of what is good for children. It also points out the directions for further research and questioning.

This study represents a solid starting point for an expanded social discussion of what work should and should not mean in the lives of today's British children, and of what public sector policies are required to guarantee them both protection and opportunity. It is also internationally significant, for its focus on the specifics of the British experience makes it a methodological example deserving attention from other countries considering similar in-depth studies of their own situation. It is, all in all, a big step in a needed direction.

William E Myers
27 August 1997

William E Myers has been involved with child work issues since 1981. He has worked for the International Labour Office and is currently a consultant to UNICEF. He has contributed to a number of books on child labour and has co-authored a just completed book entitled *What works for working children*.

List of Tables and Figures

Table 2.1	Percentage of children *ever* working prior to minimum school-leaving age.	30
Table 2.2	Working at age 15.	31
Table 2.3	Working at earlier ages.	33
Table 2.4	Best estimates of children working.	33
Table 2.5	Percentages ever worked and currently working: Scotland S4.	35
Table 2.6	Percentages ever worked and currently working: England Year 10.	35
Table 2.7	Percentages ever worked and currently working: England Year 11.	35
Table 2.8	Comparison of percentages.	36
Table 3.1	Extent of work experience: percentages.	39
Table 3.2	Main types of jobs.	41
Table 3.3	Job categories: percentages.	44
Table 3.4	Hours worked per week: percentages.	45
Table 3.5	Hours worked per week in other studies: percentages.	46
Table 3.6	Start and finish times: percentages.	46
Table 3.7	Cumbrian start and finish times: percentages.	47
Table 3.8	Hourly and weekly earnings: averages.	48
Table 3.9	Hourly earnings: percentages.	48
Table 3.10	Hourly earnings by age: averages.	49
Table 3.11	Male and female participation.	51
Table 3.12	Work status by sex: percentages.	51
Table 3.13	Job types by sex: percentages	52
Table 3.14	Job type and sex: other studies.	53
Table 3.15	Hours worked per week by sex.	53
Table 3.16	Hourly earnings by sex: percentages.	54
Table 3.17	Percentage of children who ever had a work permit.	56
Table 3.18	Percentages reporting accidents at work.	58
Table 3.19	Percentages reporting accidents at work: other findings.	58
Table 3.20	Accidents by type of job: percentages.	60
Table 4.1	Students receiving free school meals and clothing grants 1993/94 : percentages.	63
Table 4.2	School students in Year 10 surveys.	64
Table 4.3	Students in Year 11 and Year 12 surveys.	65
Table 4.4	Composition of samples.	65
Table 4.5	Work status of Year 10 students: percentages.	69
Table 4.6	Types of jobs currently undertaken by Year 10 students: percentages.	70
Table 4.7	Types of jobs currently undertaken by Year 10 students: percentages in each school.	71
Table 4.8	Hours worked per week by Year 10 students: percentages.	72

Table 4.9	Start and finish times of Year 10 students: percentages.	72
Table 4.10	Average earnings.	73
Table 4.11	Students reporting having had an accident at work: percentages.	74
Table 4.12	Breakdown of job type by gender.	75
Table 4.13	Work status of students in surveyed school years: percentages.	76
Table 5.1	Extent of work experience: percentages.	80
Table 5.2	Work and attendance: percentages.	81
Table 5.3	Work and English performance.	81
Table 5.4	Work and Mathematics performance.	82
Table 5.5	Commitment to education measures.	84
Table 5.6	Work and attendance: percentages.	84
Table 5.7	Work and return to school in S5: percentages.	84
Table 5.8	Work and academic performance.	85
Table 5.9	Start and finish times and academic performance.	86
Table 5.10	Start and finish times and commitment to education.	86
Table 5.11	Work and academic performance.	88
Table 5.12	Work and attendance.	89
Table 5.13	Work and return to Year 12.	89
Table 5.14	Hours worked and performance.	89
Table 5.15	Work status.	90
Table 5.16	Work status and performance.	90
Table 5.17	Work status and attendance.	91

Figures

Figure 7.1	Examples of costs and benefits of child employment.	137
Figure 7.2	Role of the researcher.	139
Figure 7.3	Two-way channels of influence.	139

INTRODUCTION

'What is your research about?'
'Child labour in modern Britain.'
The authors of this book have experienced so many blank looks and puzzled stares following exchanges such as this that some sort of general explanation seems necessary before presenting the reader with arguments and evidence.

Why should anyone be surprised at such a research topic? We must assume that, unless one has a specialized academic or professional interest in a subject, one's impression of it is often moulded by the mass media. Let us consider one or two articles where the issue of child labour has appeared.

Under the headline 'Concern for millions used in child labour', *The Scotsman* newspaper of 10 June 1996 quoted the director of the International Labour Organization as saying 'Today's child worker will be tomorrow's uneducated and untrained adult, forever trapped in grinding poverty.' Burkina Faso and Kenya were cited as countries with a particularly high proportion of children in their workforces. The numbers of children working in the ex-communist countries of Eastern Europe were rising. Britain was mentioned in passing. A few weeks later, another Scottish newspaper, the *Sunday Mail* (21 July 1996) carried an article headed 'Guard duty: night shift on the site for boys, 13'. The title virtually tells the story. At a building site in Glasgow, 13-year-old boys were being employed as security guards overnight.

The *Sunday Mail*, on 6 April 1997, carried another item on what it termed an 'Under-age worker scandal'. Again the title tells much of the story: 'Kid skipped school to work a 50-hour week at top hotel'. The newspaper claimed to have evidence that children were working until 11.30 p.m. (which is illegal) serving alcohol (which is also illegal). A day or two later, *The Guardian* newspaper (11 April 1997) carried an item 'Reebok and Nike pledge to improve "sweatshops"'. Leading American companies were said to be bowing to consumer pressure and drafted a charter for workers' rights in Third World countries, including not employing children under the age of 15.

Examples of both types of article could be multiplied many times over. A selection is to be found in Appendix 2. Together they may help to create a common picture of what child labour is, a large and serious problem in economically underdeveloped countries but so unusual in Britain as to warrant sensational headlines when uncovered here.

This book grows out of several years of research based at the University of Paisley. The fundamental assumption of the research is that we cannot take it for granted that this commonsense stereotype of child employment in Britain is correct. We felt the need to ask basic questions such as how many children in Britain have jobs, what are these jobs, are they good or bad for the children? We found that there was little in the way of hard evidence already available to answer these questions. Child labour was not a topic which was receiving much attention from researchers.

We do not claim to have definitive answers to these questions yet. However, the research which we have been carrying out does get us closer to reasoned answers than was possible a few years ago. We have faced certain difficulties in carrying out our enquiries, the most fundamental of which has been funding. Although in this book we have tried to bring our findings together in an organized fashion, we have to stress that this book is not the outcome of an organized, pre-planned programme of research.

We have received financial support from a variety of sources, but in many cases we have had to fit the research to the special interests of the sponsors. As a result of the preliminary work of Michael Lavalette, then a research student at Paisley, and the interest aroused by the short report on child labour published by the Scottish Low Pay Unit (Lavalette et al., 1991), we were able to persuade the University to provide some start-up funds. Two local authorities in England, Cumbria and North Tyneside, then invited us to look at the extent and nature of child employment in their areas. Since the initial research in Scotland focused on urban areas, the Scottish Low Pay Unit then sponsored an investigation into a rural area, Dumfries and Galloway. The Scottish Office Education Department provided us with a small grant to explore the impact of work on schooling and Cumbria County Council invited us to undertake a follow-up study, which also looked at the school–work relationship. All of this work was undertaken in collaboration with our research assistant Sandra Lindsay. More recently, in collaboration with Michael Lavalette, now at the University of Liverpool, we have undertaken a further investigation for an English local authority, Blackburn. The findings from these various investigations are incorporated into this book. We have also received funding from the International Working Group on Child Labour to report on child labour in Britain, Europe and the United States. Although that work is not directly reported here, it has brought us into contact with evidence and ideas which no doubt colour our approach in this book. The study of more senior pupils in Scottish schools, referred to briefly in Chapter 7, was funded by the Nuffield Foundation.

The main method we have employed in the research around which this book is organized has been the questionnaire. It may be that some readers will wish to concentrate on what we found and leave aside any consideration of how we found it. However, we do wish to emphasize that although we have used the same principal research tool as most other researchers in this field, the questionnaire method has its limitations. For that reason, caution must be exercised in interpreting our results. Our various sponsors were paying for the research from tight budgets; in the case of the local authorities they needed to have a reasonable basis on which to estimate the extent of the problems in their areas. Questionnaires can be administered quickly and cheaply. That is why they were used. However, reliance on the answers given presupposes good memories and good will on the part of those answering. Although we believe that the great majority of pupils answering our questions were cooperative and responded honestly and we have no particular reason to suspect their memories when they were dealing with the past, it would have been greatly preferable if we had had the resources to check the outcome by recourse to other research techniques. We have employed some other techniques, too, and the possibilities available to cross-check questionnaire findings with other evidence are discussed towards the end of the book.

Chapter 1 raises some of the fundamental issues which make child employment important and places British child labour in an international context. Chapter 2 reviews the evidence, partly collected by others, partly collected by ourselves on how common child employment is in Britain. Chapters 3, 4 and 5 present the main findings of our own research. First, in Chapter 3 we look at work by 14- and 15-year-olds in the five areas we have researched. Chapter 4 focuses on Cumbria, because we were able to study children in four schools over three successive years giving us a much fuller picture than the snapshot methods employed in other areas. Chapter 5 reviews the three different studies which look at the school performance and attitudes to education of workers and non-workers. Chapter 6 looks broadly at what the costs and benefits of child employment may be. The concluding chapter looks at policy issues and where research needs to go from here.

The help of many people who made the research possible must be acknowledged. First, we shall mention the school students who took the trouble to answer our questions. Sometimes they may have found it difficult to understand the point of it all, occasionally they may have even been suspicious (after all many were actually reporting that they had broken the law). The staff of the schools must also be thanked, in part for putting up with the disruption to their normal regimes, but also for searching out attendance records and examination results. The research could not have been carried out without funding and we extend our thanks to all of the bodies already listed above. Finally, we thank our working colleagues. Many contributed in minor ways to our work, but we must particularly acknowledge our original collaborator, Michael Lavalette, and Sandra Lindsay, joint author of the many technical reports from which Chapters 3, 4 and 5 derive. An earlier review of the extent of child employment in Britain was published in the *British Journal of Education and Work* (Hobbs et al., 1996a) and we are grateful to the editor for permission to use some of the material which had already appeared there.

Chapter 1

CHILD EMPLOYMENT: SOME ISSUES

INITIAL QUESTIONS

This book is about children and it is about work. We use the words 'child' and 'work' as part of everyday conversation. They are familiar and unproblematic elements in our vocabularies. Or rather, it may be more accurate to say that they usually cause us no problems. In undertaking the research which we shall describe in later chapters, we have learnt to treat these words with caution. We have grown suspicious of unthinking references to children and work. The unconsidered use of these words often carries assumptions of which the speaker is unaware and which he or she may not intend.

'Child' and 'work' are both words with long and varied usage in English. 'Child' occupies six columns of the *Oxford English Dictionary*, even if we exclude related terms such as 'childhood' and 'childish'. However, 'work', partly because it is both a noun and a verb, far outdoes this with 28 columns, excluding related words such as 'worker' and 'working'.

One reason for referring to a historical dictionary is to remind ourselves that words are constantly changing their meanings. At different times in the development of the English language the word 'child' has been employed to refer variously to a newly born infant, to a girl baby, to a young person of either sex before the age of puberty, to a youth entering manhood, to a chorister, a lad or 'boy' in service, a page, an attendant. Note that in these latter cases, the individual referred to is defined through some sort of job. This list is merely a selection of some of the meanings identified by the *Oxford English Dictionary*. Given this history, we do well not to assume that the meaning of the word 'child' is straightforward and obvious. Even such an apparently simple issue as age has its complications. Are we to look for a division between childhood and adulthood or is there a tripartite split between child, adolescent and adult? Whichever we decide, we find difficulty in reaching a decision on where in years of age to draw distinctions. Some might argue that it depends on the individual, in other words how mature that person is. This may well be a sound argument, but it makes drawing the line harder. Later in this book, we shall be reporting research in which we define child arbitrarily as someone who has not yet reached the legally set minimum age for leaving school.

This is relatively precise, but it can also give rise to the objection that few would refer to 15-year-olds as 'children' nowadays.

The Convention on the Rights of the Child adopted by the General Assembly of the United Nations in 1989 defines a child as a person 'below the age of eighteen years unless, under the law applicable to the child, majority is attained earlier'.

The United Kingdom expressed reservations about Article 32 when ratifying the Convention. British legislation on child employment distinguished between two categories of people under 18 years of age, 'children' by which broadly speaking is meant individuals who have not yet reached minimum school-leaving age and 'young persons', which refers to those over the minimum age for leaving school. The International Labour Organization, which is affiliated to the United Nations, sets 15 years as an appropriate minimum age for entering the labour force, and 18 years as the minimum age if the work is hazardous. Thus the work of those whom the United Nations regard as 'children' are differentiated on grounds of age by both national and international bodies.

Turning to the meanings of the word 'work' we would draw attention to two in particular. Work may refer to 'what a person has to do, employment'; it may also refer to 'any action requiring effort'. There is also a use of the term 'work' in which its meaning is seen as a contrast to something else called 'play'. 'Play' is another English word with many meanings. However, the work–play dichotomy is generally employed to contrast something which is imposed and onerous (work) with something which is freely chosen and enjoyable (play). Some writers (e.g. Greene and Lepper, 1974; Iso-Ahola, 1980; Lepper and Greene, 1975) have developed this contrast further in discussing parents' attitudes to children's games. They suggest that children get intrinsic pleasure from playing games. However, if parents take too obvious an interest in their child's performance in competitive games by giving a lot of advice and directions and by reacting strongly to victory and defeat, this may interfere with the child's enjoyment. By imposing extrinsic rewards and sanctions, the adults are said by these writers to 'turn play into work'. This issue itself is an important one, but we doubt whether a great deal is to be gained by applying the term 'work' to children's sport, particularly when there is another distinguishable area of childhood activity which is generally referred to as work. We are referring to economic activity.

There is little doubt that when child labour is discussed, there will be some sort of product or service which is given a monetary value. Some cases are straightforward. A child enters into a contract with an employer and receives money in return for services rendered in a factory, farm, shop or restaurant. But what if the parent receives the money and the child nothing? What if the employer is the child's parent? What if the child assists a parent in work, but receives no monetary reward? We shall have to return to such questions later. In the meantime, we ask the reader not to decide too readily what 'work' means when talking of a child.

The focus of this book is to be on children in contemporary Britain. As will be seen, we have most to say about children who attend school as well as working. However, we believe that what we have discovered from our research on these children is best interpreted if it is placed in a wider context. Accordingly, in this chapter we shall take a look back into the history of child employment in Britain and also, before that, consider some examples of child labour in other parts of the world today.

To some readers it may seem strange that this last subject is not the whole concern of this book. Many people are vaguely aware that in some countries children work in dreadful conditions for little or no wages. A number of excellent television documentaries have brought this global problem to our attention (see Appendix 1). It is difficult to watch some of these programmes without a sense of outrage. Our purpose here is not to add to that outrage, however justifiable it may be, but to look analytically at the various circumstances which can be termed 'child labour'.

CHILD LABOUR AROUND THE WORLD TODAY

The International Labour Organization (ILO) (1996) estimates that around 73 million children aged between 10 and 14 are working around the world today. There are some cases of children under 10 years of age working and the ILO did not include in its calculations girls engaged in domestic labour, so these figures are conservative. Obviously each child is an individual with his or her own needs and aspirations and his or her own problems. Equally obviously, we cannot know all of these children individually. Essentially, statistics such as those provided by the ILO are merely an aid to our understanding. No one can know for sure whether there are say 800,000 or 900,000 children working as carpet weavers in the Indian sub-continent. In a sense the precise figure doesn't matter. What the estimates tell us is that this is a substantial problem. If the estimates were 800 or 900, then it would be a less substantial problem. Let us put aside statistics for a time and look at some individual cases.

For most of them, we shall employ a slightly fictionalized presentation, but we shall start with one case where the child's real name can be employed. One reason is that this Pakistani boy has already achieved international fame. The other reason for using his real name is that since, tragically, he is now dead, he does not need the protection of anonymity we give to the living (Reddy, 1996). At the age of four, Iqbal Masih's father sold him to carpet manufacturers for the sum of 13,000 rupees. For six years he worked around 16 hours per day at a carpet loom. He received no education and his physical growth was impaired by malnourishment and restricted opportunities for exercise. In 1992, this type of work having been declared illegal by the Supreme Court of Pakistan, Iqbal Masih participated in demonstrations against the carpet makers. With the help of the Bonded Labour

Liberation Front, he was freed from his job and taken to Lahore. An appearance on American television networks in 1994 made him a symbol of the struggle against child-bonded labour. His progress at school was so rapid that the International Bonded Labour Foundation presented him with the Reebok Prize for outstanding performance. On 16 April 1996, during a visit to his home village, a few miles from Lahore, Iqbal Masih was shot dead. Disputes arose about the circumstances of his murder. One claim was that he had been shot by a farm labourer whom he had disturbed committing a crime. However, given his prominence, it is not surprising that some commentators suggested that it had been a political assassination. The Carpet Manufacturers Association of Lahore denied any involvement. However, whatever the truth of the matter, his death brought substantial publicity to the cause with which he had been associated.

Iqbal is someone whose story made the headlines. However, its dramatic nature may mislead us. He may represent a specific problem in a specific part of the world at a specific time. We need to look at child workers more broadly. The case histories which follow are based on real children but names and some trivial identifying details have been changed.

Alfredo

Alfredo is 13 years old. He lives in a small town in northern Portugal. Every day from 8.00 a.m. to 7.30 p.m. he works with his father as a stonebreaker. They trim paving stones destined to be exported and used in shopping precincts in many parts of the world, including Britain. He has done this since he left school two years ago, before he had reached the official school-leaving age in Portugal, which is 12 years of age. His father did the same when he was a boy. He would have liked Alfredo to have had an education with some prospect of a better job, but did not see this as a realistic possibility. Alfredo's father has a bad cough, which he knows is caused by years of working in an atmosphere contaminated by stone dust. He fears that Alfredo, too, will eventually show the ill effects of these working conditions. Alfredo's older sister works too, at a local shoe factory, known locally as 'the crèche', because most of the employees are working children. Apologists explain the high level of child labour in this part of Portugal as a cultural phenomenon, since children have 'always' worked. Alfredo's father has another explanation, poverty.

David

David is a 13-year-old Welsh boy with what he considers a 'job' at a holiday camp. He helps guests when they arrive and depart by carrying their luggage. Although the law requires him to have a work permit, like most of the 40 or so other young people he works with, David does not have one. If he were to have an accident, it seems uncertain whether he would be covered by the company's employee insurance policy. This is particularly so because the company does not consider David an 'employee' at all. Their clinching argument is that they do not pay him. David and the other young people who carry luggage rely exclusively on tips. As if to further distance themselves from the luggage carriers, the holiday camp company claim that they do not advertise this as a service to customers. However, David and his colleagues congregate by a sign reading 'Luggage Porters Available Here'. The guests' cases are heavy. The work is out of doors. The company provides its adult employees with waterproof clothing. Since David and the other porters are not regarded as employees by the company, those who run the {$liday camp do nothing to protect them against the elements nor do they attempt to control the weights these young people pull or carry.

Ion

Ion is 11 years old. He is one of an estimated 1,400 'street children' in Bucharest, the capital of Romania. Like most of them, he is a member of a group living in the area of the North Railway Station. Others are centred on central area underground stations. Ion has attended school, but only for two years. Not surprisingly, therefore, when he comes into contact with social workers they record that he is expressing words incorrectly and with difficulty. He sometimes sleeps in the station waiting room, but does not really have a secure and regular rest place. Usually he cannot get enough sleep. That is why he looks pale and tired most of the time, and is prone to illness. Ion earns money in any way he can, even illegally. This may include begging for money and food. Occasionally, he gets a casual job such as unloading a lorry. He has some slight contact with his family, returning home from time to time. However, the last trip home was over a year ago, so like many other children he may soon break off all relations with his family and with the social welfare bodies. His reasons for leaving home in the first place included the fact that his father had an alcohol problem. In effect, on the street Ion has created a new family, the group of children who live like himself. The group is structured as a 'business society' in which the social division of labour operates, each member having a well-defined role, in accordance with their personal talent and skills for earning money. Some children specialize in stealing, others in begging. The cohesion within the group is high, due to the need for protection against attacks from other groups or from the police. Ion pays a 'protection' fee to the older group members. For sometime now, Ion has been inhaling solvents. Recently he moved on to a drug called locally 'aurolac'.

Errol

Errol is 14; he lives in Marmaris, Turkey. His family migrated from another part of Turkey in the hope of getting work in the developing tourist trade. His father works as a driver for 'safari tours'. In the summer of his first year in high school, Errol worked as a bar boy at a place run by his sister and her husband. He did mainly cleaning work and also learned a lot about cocktails during this first work experience. He observed the barman's style of work very closely and aspired to be like him. He tasted the left-overs in the shaker to learn about cocktails. At the end of summer, he felt that he had no chance of entering the university, so he decided to leave school. He now works as a barman during the tourist season. He works 14 hours a day, starting early and finishing late, with a break during the day. In the off season, he is enrolled as an apprentice at the Tourism and Hotel Management Training Centre in Marmaris. He is unhappy at work because he is getting a low rating for tips. The amount collected in the tip-box is shared on the basis of a rating system, he explained. He thinks that, because of his age, he has been rated lower than what he deserved. Inhabitants of Marmaris are conservative people but very tolerant towards tourists. Like other apprentices he thinks that it would be a good idea to marry a foreign girl and go abroad. He has had several foreign girlfriends, he tells people, all of them older than himself.

Fatima

Fatima is eight years old. She lives in the Nile delta of Egypt. She is one of many children in Egypt who, whenever they can, work rather than go to school. Her local school is overcrowded. The lessons do not seem to lead to any knowledge that will help her in later life. The teacher, who is poorly trained and poorly paid, cannot really cope with the large class. Fatima works as a jasmine picker. Jasmine is used in the preparation of expensive perfumes, though Fatima is paid very little. This is despite the fact that in a sense the children are regarded as having unique skill. Their small hands can pick the jasmine without the danger of damage which exists if the blossoms are removed by a larger adult hand. To maximize the retention of the jasmine essence, the picking takes place at night. A lorry carries the pickers to the fields at 1.00 a.m. They work till dawn under the supervision of an overseer carrying a stick with which he beats any picker who works too slowly or misses some blossoms.

Bonnie

Bonnie is five years old and lives in Tennessee. So far she has won over ten thousand dollars and a car at child beauty pageants. She began when she was nine months old. Now, in elaborate clothes and make-up, she sings and parades before the judges. At first she took part in small local events but, to quote her grandmother, 'We go for the big money now.' The grandmother runs a beauty parlour. Bonnie's mother is a former adult model. Together they plot Bonnie's schedule, with the aid of *Pageant* magazine. They have entered Bonnie in the Southern Charm Pageant in Atlanta, Georgia, which they consider highly prestigious even though it does not offer the highest prizes. Bonnie will also be taking part in another pageant in Louisville, Kentucky. There are five cars among the prizes and 'Grandma needs a car.' Bonnie's father supports his wife and mother-in-law's plans for Bonnie, but he has some reservations. 'It's tough,' he says, 'We push her a little bit; sometimes

I'd like her to be just a kid.' Bonnie has a specially built rehearsal stage with full-length mirrors in her play room. She takes singing, acting and modelling lessons. She has cosmetic false teeth because the judges put a lot of emphasis on having a good smile. Bonnie's mother and grandmother seem unaware that anyone might criticize what they admit is almost like a full-time job. Pageant organizers and judges are more used to answering negative comments: 'To do this for your child you have to really love them.'

Sanji

Sanji is eight years old. His home is in a small village in north-east India. Everyone in his village is extremely poor, so there was a lot of interest when a carpet manufacturer came with an offer of work. Children were required to weave carpets in another village some distance away. Each child's parent would be given a basic payment of 300 rupees. The children would go off by train, would be entertained by being shown films and could weave for good piece-work rates. They understood that they would be allowed to work when they felt able and to rest when they were tired. Sanji and several other children went off happy, worried only about the possibility of becoming homesick. Communications between poor people in distant villages is difficult in this part of India. Sanji's parents heard nothing of their son for several months. Then his father heard a rumour that Sanji was ill. Worried for his son, he spent the last of his cash on medicine and a train ticket. When he arrived at the carpet manufacturer's village, he found Sanji and the other village children living in squalor. They were made to work more than 16 hours a day, fed little and frequently beaten. They were dirty and their bodies covered in sores. Sanji's father said he was going to take the children back to their home village, but the carpet boss said that he had invested 500 rupees in each child. He demanded that this be repaid before he would allow the children to go.

Ana

Ana is 13 years old. She lives in a poor district of Bahia, Brazil. Her mother finds it difficult to get work, so Ana helps out as best she can. One opportunity to earn a little money is when tourists flock to the religious festivals such as the Feast of Santa Barbara. Ana sells ribbons like many other girls. According to Ana, on a couple of occasions when she couldn't sell enough ribbons, she had sex with tourists. However, ribbon selling is a well-recognized way in which local girls can make contact with tourists in the hope of getting clothes or money in exchange for sex. When Ana's mother discovered she had been sleeping with men, she tried unsuccessfully to stop her ribbon selling. Ana is illiterate. She feels that if she could learn to read she could give up her way of life (she doesn't call it prostitution) and do something more worth while with her life.

Juanito

Juanito is six years old. His parents, from a poor background in Mexico, went to California in the hope of finding work and a better standard of living. His father became a migrant agricultural worker. One regular job has been garlic picking. However, over a five-year period, the rate of pay offered by the employers has fallen year by year. In order to accumulate a living wage Juanito's father has to have his family, including Juanito, work in the fields with him, picking and trimming the garlic. Juanito's earning capacity works out at about a dollar for a long day's work. What Juanito is doing is illegal but there are seldom any checks made on whether children are working. If an inspection is to be made, the employers ensure that Juanito and the other children are out of sight until the inspectors have gone.

The children on whom these case histories have been based were not chosen to be representative of working children world wide. Nor have they been chosen to stress the extreme evils of child labour, otherwise we would have included children who are soldiers or the inmates of brothels. What we are attempting to do is illustrate at least some of the variety of circumstances in which work is a significant part of a child's life. Let us note some of the variations.

The most obvious variable to the reader may be a moral one, in other words the extent to which one is ethically repelled by the child's situation. It might be argued, for example, that carrying heavy cases in the rain (David) or working as a barman for part of the year and being trained for the rest (Errol) are relatively positive working roles compared with forced carpet weaving (Sanji) and prostitution (Ana). Similarly, it might be argued that how one reacts to full-time participation in beauty pageants (Bonnie) is largely a matter of culturally created assumptions and expectations. We believe that, if we are concerned with ways of helping children, we need to put some of our moral judgements aside temporarily, to explore the circumstances more analytically.

Let us consider economic aspects. One common belief is that child labour is brought about by poverty. Poverty clearly plays a part in many of these cases. Alfredo left school because of poverty. Fatima would presumably not work in the fields if the family didn't need the money. Sanji and his parents were tricked through their desperation to escape from grinding poverty. Juanito works because without his aid the family cannot achieve a living wage. Ana, too, is selling ribbons and sex because of her poverty. However, in other cases, the circumstances seem less clear cut. Ion may have come to live on the streets because of poverty, but he blames his father's alcohol abuse, which might in turn be seen as arising from poverty, of course. Errol seems to have made a reasoned choice for work rather than high school. Bonnie's parents are comfortably off, certainly by the standards of most of these other children's families. About David, we just don't know. Child labour is associated with poverty, but it is too simple-minded to assume that, with the elimination of poverty, child labour will automatically die out. Errol and Ana were not equally poor, but both seem to have been drawn to the world of tourism. The appeal of luxury consumer products and of apparently attractive life styles may well play a major part in inducing children to work.

This gives rise to another question, that of personal choice. It might be argued that Bonnie and Sanji, for example, represent two extremes, with Bonnie expressing herself as keen to be a pageant girl and Sanji feeling he has been tricked into slavery. However, we must avoid making too ready judgements about the children making choices. Bonnie participated in pageants before she could speak. She has no experience of *not* being a competitor in pageants. Did Alfredo 'choose' to cut stones when he became 12 years old? His family is poor. His father had done so when he was a boy. Did he feel he could do otherwise. What could Ana 'choose' to do if she were to decide not to sell ribbons? In almost all of these cases, we would suggest, it is much easier to see the force of economic or cultural circumstances at work than acts of choosing.

Let us explore economic relationships in which the children are involved a little more precisely. The everyday concept of a 'job' is that one undertakes some sort of activity on a regular basis and in return receives a regular payment. Alfredo, Errol and Fatima regularly cut stones, serve drink and pick jasmine, respectively, for a wage. However, Ana and Ion get paid only for irregularly contracted deals; David is paid tips; Bonnie may or may not win a prize. Juanito is 'paid' only indirectly in that his efforts contribute to the family's total wage. Sanji, who works the longest of all these children, receives no wage and only an inadequate ration of food.

Another way to look at the work is to consider in what way it is economically productive. Alfredo and Sanji help to produce artifacts, paving stones and carpets respectively. Jasmine and Juanito take part in harvesting. The others provide various sorts of service, in three cases (Ana, Errol and David) these are linked to the tourist trade.

How is the family involved in the work? It is not always clear. The attitudes of the families of David and Ion are uncertain. Bonnie's parents encourage her work and plan it, but for the parents of Alfredo, Jasmine and Juanito, the fact that their children work seems a painful necessity. Sanji's father initially approved of his working, until he discovered the real conditions in which his labour would be exploited. Ana's mother does not want her to have sex with tourists, but seems powerless to stop her.

What of the varying effects the work may have on the children? Sanji's work as a carpet weaver clearly endangers his health, as does Alfredo's work as a stone trimmer. Ion is also at risk, but more from the overall life style of the 'street child' than from the work which he does. David may be carrying luggage which is too heavy for him. The others do not seem to have specific health hazards, unless one includes venereal diseases in the case of Ana.

A common objection to child employment is that it interferes with the child's education. Errol and Alfredo gave up school in order to work, but in Errol's case there is the compensation of being at a training centre for part of the year. Bonnie and Juanito are still relatively young. One could envisage them going through conventional schooling later, though the middle-class Bonnie seems to have a much better chance of that than the Mexican migrant, Juanito. Ion's loss of contact with school is part of the process whereby he is alienated from 'normal' society. However, the schooling on offer for Fatima is not of a sort that we can necessarily say that she is disadvantaging herself by missing it. Sanji, of course, lost the opportunity to attend school when he became, in effect, part of a forced labour force. However, educational opportunities in his village were extremely limited. David's position is unclear on the evidence available. He goes to school, but we do not know how well he does or whether the work affects his performance at school or his commitment to education. It is to people like David that attention will be paid in later chapters.

What of the children's futures? For most of them the prospects of a happy, fulfilling adulthood seem small. Errol may come to own his own bar, Bonnie may become a model or own a beauty parlour, but otherwise one would be hard put to make a realistic favourable prediction for any of the others. However, with the exception of Sanji and Alfredo, whose health may have been damaged by their work and whose prospects for a favourable adult life style may thereby have been reduced, it is hard to be sure how large a part work, as such, plays in moulding each child's future. Ion lives rough and takes drugs; compared to these factors the effect of the work he does seems likely to be relatively trivial. If steps had been taken to stop Juanito, Fatima, Ana and David from working, could we expect them to have a better life as adults? In each case the family income would have been that little bit less, but it is unclear that the time which would otherwise have been spent working would be used in a way which would prepare them for a more successful adult life. This is not because of any inner failing of these children but because of lack of opportunity.

CHILD LABOUR IN BRITAIN IN THE PAST

If, as we have suggested, children work in a variety of economic and cultural settings, and for a variety of economic and cultural reasons, then a study of children in Britain today requires us to contextualize their work. Just as some people in Britain think of child labour today as essentially a problem for certain other countries, so it is common to think of child labour in Britain as a thing of the past. Many of us are aware that the Industrial Revolution led to many children working in factories, mills and mines. Many are aware, too, that British children once climbed up inside chimneys to clean them. However, there is probably a widespread view that, as a result of the campaigns of philanthropists such as Lord Shaftesbury and as a result of the establishment of a system of compulsory education, child employment has not existed on any substantial scale for a century. Evidence against such a rosy view will be found in the subsequent chapters of this book. However, it is instructive to look back into our past to examine just what has happened to child employment in the period since the Industrial Revolution.

The Industrial Revolution in Britain is seen as a time when large numbers of children, many of them quite young, became involved in economic production. There have been many disputes about what this involved for the children themselves, what aspects were beneficial and what aspects were harmful. One problem which arises in trying to understand the lives of children at that period is that it is difficult to compare what they experienced then with what children of previous generations had experienced. It is clear that child labour was not invented during the Industrial Revolution. Children had worked before, in the home and on the farm, for example. What such work involved is difficult to pin down, however, because few writers of the time thought it worthy of description or comment. That children had become involved in industrial production before the classic period of the Industrial Revolution (late 18th and early 19th centuries) is clear from Daniel Defoe's *Tour Through the Whole Island of Great Britain* in 1724. However, describing with approval children at work in Taunton, Somerset, Defoe remarked he had seen this in only one other place in England, namely Colchester in Essex. Either Defoe was ill-informed, or child work was largely domestic or agricultural at that time (Lavalette, 1994).

Once the Industrial Revolution got underway, it soon became common for children to work, but it would be wrong to assume that the circumstances were identical for all. Some children were employed in large mills or factories, but in varying ways. In some cases, they might be in the same building or workshop as their parents; in others they might be separated from their families. Pauper children might be sent to mills built in previously remote spots where adult workers were scarce. Some aspects of textile production still took place in workers' homes, where children might assist a parent or employer. It would not have been difficult to find in Britain, at that time, the equivalents of Iqbal, Sanji, Alfredo and some of the others we described above.

Although many accounts of the lives of working children may make us look back in horror, it has been argued that, at the time, this type of work would not have seemed especially hard to the children themselves or the adults around, because they knew that life had been hard before the factories came. This view is expressed, for example by Hutt (1954), who also argued that had children not been engaged in production they would not have had any alternative useful way of filling their time. E. P. Thompson, in his book, *The Making of the English Working Class* (1968), acknowledged that children had previously worked within the family, and that the work may have often been onerous. However, he believed that as far as children were concerned, the factory system had all of the evils of domestic labour and none of the compensations. In particular, factory work was more monotonous and more continuous than the work children had typically undertaken in earlier times.

The anonymous autobiography *Chapters in the Life of a Dundee Factory Boy* (1951, first published 1850) conveys something of the experience of the young worker in the mill and suggests the appropriateness of Thompson's analysis.

> When I went to a spinning mill I was about seven years of age. I had to get out of bed every morning at five o'clock, commence work at half past five, drop at nine for breakfast, begin again at half-past nine, work until two, which was the dinner hour, start again at half-past two, and continue until half-past seven at night. Such were the nominal hours; but in reality there were no regular hours, masters and managers did with us as they liked. (p. 11)

> About a week after I became a mill boy, I was seized with a strong, heavy sickness that few escape on first becoming factory workers. The cause of the illness, which is known by the name of the 'mill fever', is the pestiferous atmosphere produced by so many breathing in a confined space, together with the heat and the exhalations of grease and oil ... This fever does not often lay the patient up. It is slow, dull, and painfully wearisome in its operation. It produces a sallow and debilitated look, destroys rosy cheeks, and unless the constitution be very strong, leaves its pale impress for life. (p. 14)

> At that time mill-masters did not employ men for rousing their hands in the morning ... I wish I knew the benevolent person who first conceived and carried into execution the plan of warning them each morning ... The plan at once removed a load of anxiety and pain off the minds of the young, as the terror of sleeping in kept them in a nightly state of unhappiness ... We had no clock in the house, and my mother used to rise at all hours of the night, and sit until she heard the Cowgate clock strike an hour. Often has she sat from a little past three until five, when she would waken me and return to her bed. (p. 26)

The debates among 20th-century historians mirror arguments which took place at the time of the Industrial Revolution itself, except of course that in the 19th century these were live issues of great practical significance. A number of figures are remembered today as champions of the factory child, often in opposition of owners and managers, who found ways of justifying virtually every practice.

Richard Oastler (1789–1861), a flamboyant campaigner, is said to have dedicated himself to the cause of child workers at the request of a reforming factory owner. He began in 1830, by publishing a letter entitled 'Yorkshire Slavery' in the newspaper *Leeds Mercury*. In 1833 he addressed the first meeting on the plight of factory children to be held in London. His opponents, who nicknamed him the 'factory king', became particularly incensed when he appeared to threaten that he would teach children to use their grandmothers' knitting needles to sabotage factory machinery.

Robert Owen (1771–1858), a man of shrewd financial and managerial skills, came to dedicate himself to philanthropy, trade unionism and socialism. When he took charge of the New Lanark mills in Scotland, he found the workforce included almost five hundred pauper 'apprentices' aged between 5 and 10 years old. Owen gradually replaced them by older children working as 'free labourers', for whom he provided educational and recreational facilities. He began to campaign publicly for children of under 10 to be excluded from factory work and for restrictions on the hours worked by older children, publishing, for example, *On the Employment of Children in Manufactories* in 1818.

For Lord Shaftesbury (1801–85) a life-long dedication to Evangelical Christianity lay behind his many campaigns dedicated to the cause of child workers. He played a prominent part in formulating laws restricting work by children in factories, mills and mines. Shaftesbury fought a long battle to end the practice of boys climbing up chimneys to clean them, culminating in the passage in 1875 of the Chimney Sweep Act.

Such men, and others like them, are now held in high esteem for their efforts to undermine ways of treating children which almost everyone now regards as unacceptable. However, it is sometimes argued that the efforts of these well-intentioned men were less important than economic and technical factors in bringing about a decline in the extent of child labour. Most early attempts to control child labour really only related to minor details and the legislation effectively only set up a minimum age for work and conditions of work in particular trades (Cunningham, 1991). Lack of inspection frequently meant that the laws were ineffectual. However, new processes were developed which reduced the need to rely on the small and nimble fingers of children. New techniques were developed which required a more skilled workforce and factory owners began to see the advantages of 'investing' in a more educated workforce. The decline of factory work for children and the rise of compulsory education are seen as going hand in hand. They are indeed linked but the transition was slow and far from smooth.

Consider, for example, the phenomenon of Half-time Working. First introduced as a result of the Factory Acts of 1833 and 1844, Half-time Working was a system which developed as a response to the growing campaign against child labour led by philanthropists like Shaftesbury as well as the workers' own Short-time Committees. The intention was to spare children from the rigours of a full working day of, say, 15 hours and instead combine limited working with a basic education. The system was never a universal one throughout Britain but it was common within the textile industry in the cities of northern England. The legislation gave birth to a number of factory schools built within factory compounds, though they were probably seldom run as well as Owen's pioneering establishment at New

Lanark. Mill owners responded by developing the relay system where children worked a rotating shift pattern, with three children now employed sequentially to do the work previously undertaken by two. Over a 24-hour period, therefore, three children would work 8-hour shifts. In addition they attended school for 4 hours. Thus the educational requirements of the legislation did not interfere with the operation of the factories.

The control of child labour was in practice very haphazard. Half-time Working was gradually phased out by compulsory full-time education, but it remained in the textile industry until 1918 and the Education Act of that year. The 1911 Census indicates that children under 14 years provided one-sixth of the labour in the cotton industry (Frow and Frow, 1970).

The gradual introduction of compulsory education and concomitant increases in the school-leaving age had the effect of removing large numbers of children from the labour market. The Elementary Education Act of 1870 was intended to set up a system of schooling for working-class children, and provided for the appointment of the first School Attendance Officers. The schools were to provide strictly circumscribed teaching up to the school-leaving age, which, under certain bylaws, could be as early as 10 (Simon, 1965).

The provisions of the 1870 Act may seem extremely modest, but they should be judged in the light of existing conditions. Caulton (1985) cites a Sheffield cutlery worker, speaking when he was 12 years old in 1865:

> Have worked at cutlery for father for seven years. Don't know anything about the Queen or England. Don't live in England. Think it's a country, but didn't know before. There are six days in a week. There is another day; altogether it makes[after a long pause] seven days. [His father said that it was true that his boy had worked for him for seven years, but that though he flogged him to make him go to school, the boy 'would come to the shop'.]

The 1874 Factory Act raised the half-time age to 10 years old, and the 1880 Education Act made school attendance compulsory for all children between the ages of 5 and 10. Up to the age of 14 years, there could be exemptions which allowed the child to work, provided educational proficiency and previous good attendance could be demonstrated. The school-leaving age was raised to 11 years in 1893, and to 12 years in 1899. However, the introduction of compulsory education by no means nullified the demand for cheap child labour. Many children entered various unregulated forms of employment, such as street selling and 'outwork', that is subcontracted parts of some manufacturing process. Certain occupations came to be regarded as 'boys' work', service work such as messenger and van boy being examples. However, many boys were trapped in a vicious circle, as those who found steady work from the ages of 10 to 14 years tended to lose their jobs at 16 or 18. By then, because they had no formal training, they were unsuited for anything but casual work (Jones, 1976). This phenomenon became known at the time as 'the boy labour problem', and the economic conditions which encouraged it were to persist until the late 1930s.

With the growth of the practices of delivering milk to the doorstep in bottles and similar delivery of morning and evening newspapers, these, too, came to be regarded as the domain of children. In the main these were treated as part-time jobs which could be combined with school attendance.

The Employment of Children Act 1903 forbade the employment of children between 9.00 p.m. and 6.00 a.m. and banned street selling by children under 11 years of age, but the effectiveness of the measure depended on the willingness of local authorities to enforce it. During the First World War, circumstances substantially increased the demand for juvenile and child labour. School children formed an important source of labour in agricultural production, and school leavers were employed in large numbers in factories (Morrow, 1989).

Arguments about the employment of children continued throughout the war but there was a gradual acceptance that children would have to work for the war effort, even though the effects were potentially harmful to their health and education. Some school boards allowed 'holidays' for children over 12 years so they could work on the land during harvests, and reports from local education authorities showed that large and ever-increasing numbers of children were being exempted from school for agricultural work.

After the war, children under 14 continued to be legally employed half time until January 1921, when the Employment of Women, Young Persons and Children Act 1920 came into effect, prohibiting the employment of children under 14 in any 'industrial undertaking' or on board ships, with the exception of children working for their parents or as apprentices (Simon, 1965).

Successive governments during the inter-war period appear to have shown a certain amount of complacency towards work by school children. However, the 1933 Children and Young Persons Act prohibited the employment of children under 12 years of age (later amended to 13 years), during school hours, before 6.00 a.m. (later amended to 7.00 a.m.) and after 7.00 p.m., or for more than two hours on a school day or a Sunday. It also prohibited children from lifting or carrying anything potentially injurious and banned work in street trading under the age of 17. A similar Act was passed for Scotland in 1937. The Children and Young Persons Act 1933, although amended in various ways, remains the main legislative control on children's employment today.

The 1936 Education Act raised the school-leaving age to 15 years, but retained exemptions for beneficial employment from age 14 years. In any case, the Second World War intervened before the Act could be implemented. Children again provided a vital but rarely acknowledged source of labour during the Second World War. They contributed to the war effort in a number of ways, primarily in agriculture. Children continued to be employed in industrial work during the war, and school leavers and young workers were employed in large numbers in munitions and aircraft factories, often working extremely long hours. Every year during the war, the Board of Education called on local authorities to arrange for school holidays to be fixed, if necessary at short notice, in those periods when the needs for seasonal agricultural labour was greatest, so that children over 12 years of age could be employed in agricultural operations during the holidays. In addition it was expected that schools should organize parties to visit local farms on certain days in term time in order to help with the work of planting and lifting potatoes. In effect, during the Second World War, many children returned to the old half-time system, although that name was not employed (Morrow, 1989).

The 1944 Education Act and its Scottish equivalent raised the school-leaving age to 15, with no exemptions. After the war, the child employment issue appears to have become less problematic, and by the late 1950s, part-time work by school children began to be seen as having some potential educational value. See for example, the Crowther Report (Ministry of Education, 1959). Likewise, the Newsom Committee, set up in 1963 to advise on the education of pupils aged 13 to 16 of average and less-than-average ability, seems to have regarded part-time work by school children as an acceptable fact of life, if not a positive source of outside experience (Ministry of Education, 1963).

There was an acknowledgement that such out-of-school work might need to be regulated, but the 1933 Act was considered to do that. However, that Act put the onus on local authorities to ensure that the law was implemented and gave local authorities a certain amount of discretion in the formulation of bylaws. In the early 1970s a study sponsored by the Department of Health and Social Security found evidence that many children were working and that the work seemed to be having a harmful effect on their schooling. This study, by Davies (1972), will be considered in more detail later. At this point we may note, however, that it was soon followed by the Employment of Children Act of 1973, which aimed to tighten up and standardize the execution of the law. However, that law remains unimplemented.

SOME FURTHER QUESTIONS

That child labour represents a massive problem across the world today can hardly be doubted. It is equally true, that in the past child labour has been a serious social problem in Britain. But where does that leave the question of child employment in Britain as we approach the end of the 20th century. Can we regard it as a minor issue because the working Davids of Britain are faced with a less serious problem than the Sanjis, Anas, Fatimas and Alfredos who are to be found in other countries? Can we assume that the admittedly slow and halting process of legislating *against* child work and *for* child education has reduced child employment to the status of a marginal problem in Britain today?

There are a number of reasons for cautioning against such a rosy view. The first is simply the fact that until quite recently, the information available on the extent and character of child employment in Britain has been very limited. One explanation for such a state of affairs might have been that there was little work about which information could be collected. Evidence is now gradually emerging, however, and it is discussed later in this book. We shall not pre-empt here the detailed discussion which follows, but we can indicate that it appears that work by school-aged children is widespread and appears in some respects to be problematic.

Another reason for caution is the fact that we can never be sure what forces are at work which may produce an upsurge in child labour. It is not just that in both world wars Britain found it expedient to turn to children to help in the production of food and munitions. The phenomenon is wider than that; employers have frequently found it expedient to use children to do certain jobs. This applies not simply to manufacturing where children have been considered 'suitable' for certain jobs, weaving being an obvious example. It also applies to the provision of services. Across the world, children deliver, stack, serve and clean. Tourism is a large and growing industry and opportunities for children to participate are substantial.

The effect of social attitudes must also be considered. We have in mind particularly the attitudes of children and parents. One potentially significant factor is whether children themselves want to have a job. As we shall see, the evidence suggests that in the main they do. Children today are targeted by sustained marketing campaigns aimed at selling expensive consumer goods. For parents to completely protect their children from consumerism is very difficult because of the pervasive nature of the mass media. One way for them to try to counterbalance the effects of advertising is to require that the consumer goods be earned in some way. This can take different forms, doing well at school, undertaking domestic chores, and engaging in waged work.

It should also be kept in mind that support for full-time education is by no means complete. Each time the minimum school-leaving age has been raised, it has been hotly debated. The current age of 16 still has its critics, particularly on the political right. The titles of a couple of articles expressing these views are clear and unequivocal, 'Why state education is bad for children' (Scruton, 1990) and 'Why raising the school leaving age was wrong' (Sherman, 1996). Sherman claims that when the school-leaving age was last raised it meant the presence in school class rooms of boys who would have made 'good apprentices or juniors at 14' who found the lessons irrelevant. According to Sherman, the outcome was disruption and mass truancy. Scruton argues not only for the lowering of the school-leaving age but explicitly supports what he refers to as a 'Victorian value', child labour. He writes of 14-year-olds acquiring independence, responsibility and self-respect as builders' apprentices, electricians' mates and stable hands. He argues that there would be no shortage of jobs if 'the pay were sufficiently low'. Sherman calls upon Tony Blair, the then Labour Party leader and now the Prime

Minister, to acknowledge that it would be better for many working-class children to be absorbed into the world of work at 14, and claims that this view was also expressed in the 1970s by the Labour Prime Minister, James Callaghan.

It might be argued that Scruton and Sherman are not in a position of political authority and that their views are not those of the Conservative Party. However, suspicions that there might be covert intentions to encourage school pupils into the workplace have been expressed. When the pilot scheme for General National Vocational Qualifications was announced, *The Guardian* newspaper (Carvel, 1995) claimed that the Education and Employment Secretary 'moved quickly to quash reports that 14-year-olds who lost interest in school were to be sent off to work for part of the week with local firms'. Mrs Shepherd, the then Secretary, was described as pouring scorn on the 'media frenzy' which had developed. John Monks, the General Secretary of the Trades Union Congress (TUC), said that he believed 14 was too young for 'sustained work-based training' and referred to the danger of exploitation by unscrupulous employers. That children in part-time employment in Britain are already exploited by some employers has been a recurring claim of a number of bodies in recent years, including the Low Pay Network, the Labour Research Department, the GMB Union (General Municipal and Boilermakers) and the TUC itself.

In the 1980s the London-based Low Pay Unit produced two reports on extent of child labour in south-east England (MacLennan, 1982; MacLennan et al., 1985). This was followed in 1991, by a larger study of Birmingham (Pond and Searle, 1991). The Scottish Low Pay Unit and the Manchester Low Pay Unit have also published the results of regional studies (Lavalette, 1994; Lavalette et al., 1991; McKechnie et al., 1994). The Labour Research Department (1997) has drawn attention to the extent to which local authorities fail to implement the law on child employment. The GMB Union has incorporated child labour into its campaign on the rights of young workers (GMB, 1995). The TUC has commissioned a survey by MORI on child labour in England and Wales. When publishing the results (Trades Union Congress, 1997), it called for government resources to be made available to implement laws which are widely ignored at present.

Exploitation is also a recurring theme of sensational press reports on children working for low wages and in dangerous conditions. 'Child "sweat shop" probe' (*Lancashire Evening Post*, 12 April 1994), 'Boy, 15, died working in factory' (*The Guardian*, 29 March 1995), 'Hard-sell bosses hound poor Pauline, 15, after she tries to kill herself' (*Sunday Mail*, 23 June 1996), 'Guard duty: night shift on the site for boys, 13' (*Sunday Mail*, 21 July 1996). These are a fairly representative, and self-explanatory, sample.

In contrast to these claims, it is instructive to compare the approach taken to child employment by the Conservative government. That this government formulated a policy on child labour at all seems reasonably to be due to the European

Community. In 1993 after what was reported in the press as an 'extraordinary row' (McLaughlin, 1993), the then British Employment Secretary negotiated an opt-out from EC legislation controlling the maximum permissible hours of work per week for children of various ages. The Secretary, Mr David Hunt, was widely quoted as claiming to have achieved 'a great victory for the newspaper boys and girls of Britain'. He referred to British school children's 'traditional right to earn pocket money by delivering newspapers and gaining work experience from a few hours' work at weekends'. No reference was made to issues such as exploitative rates of pay, dangerous working conditions or unenforced laws. The British government's isolation on the issue was complete. When discussed in the European Parliament, their usual allies, the Christian Democrats, voted with the socialists to oppose the opt-out (Carvel, 1994). Critics claimed that the 'traditional' work that Mr Hunt claimed he was defending was not in fact under threat from EC regulations. This view seemed to be borne out when the British government began to move towards achieving compatibility when the opt-out ends. The Department of Health and the Scottish Office issued a Consultative Document which, in effect, proposed that this goal could be achieved within the existing law, if local authorities were to adopt a standardized set of bylaws. The bylaws proposed in the document offered no fundamental shift in the conception of what work should be permissible, except that rather longer hours would be permissible on a Sunday. Thus the government's position seemed to be that there was no major 'problem' of child labour in Britain. This fits neatly with the rather stereotyped picture of children's work contained in remarks of David Hunt quoted above.

It is against this background that we argue that it is worth exploring children's work in Britain today. How many children work in Britain today? How young are they when they start? What jobs do they do? How long do they work? What are they paid? Are the jobs healthy and safe? Do jobs harm school work? Do jobs aid school work? Are there other costs or benefits? Are the jobs legal? These all seem to us reasonable questions to pose. Obvious policy implications would flow depending on the answers obtained. Yet, when we began to explore child labour in Britain, we found that not one of these questions could be answered with any certainty. Today, as we hope to demonstrate in the chapters which follow, significantly more is known.

Chapter 2

THE EXTENT OF CHILD EMPLOYMENT IN BRITAIN

INTRODUCTION

In this chapter we address an apparently simple question: how many children of school age in Britain today have jobs? The answer is a matter of dispute. In the early 1990s reports of empirical studies began to appear which suggested that child employment was on quite a substantial scale; see, for example, *The Hidden Army* (Pond and Searle, 1991) and *The Forgotten Workforce* (Lavalette et al., 1991). However, the government of the time took the view that not many children had jobs and that those who did have jobs were undertaking light and acceptable tasks. For example, government minister, Michael Forsyth (Department of Employment), appearing before the House of Commons European Standing Committee B when it was considering Protection of Young People at Work, was scornful of the estimate by the Low Pay Unit (Pond and Searle, 1991) that there might be up to two million children working in Britain (House of Commons, 1993). Mr Forsyth and Tim Yeo (Department of Health) appeared before the House of Lords Select Committee on the European Communities when it was discussing the same issue, and both took a similar line of the small and essentially trivial level of child labour in Britain (House of Lords, 1993). The government's position at this time could also be found in the Department of Employment's document *The United Kingdom in Europe: People, Jobs and Progress* (1993). There was no need to introduce European measures to control child labour since Britain's tight legislative controls meant there was no major problem in this country.

The government's position relied to quite a large extent on assumptions about the extent of child employment in Britain. There were no satisfactory official figures available. Although not mentioned by the ministers concerned, a national sample survey had been organized in the summer of 1992. The results were eventually published three years later (Hibbett and Beatson, 1995). As we shall see, the findings from that study were broadly in line with those of other investigators, including those about which ministers had been so sceptical. However, before considering the results of the various investigations, including our own, it is necessary to make clear that there are still many reasons for caution when we try to estimate how many children in Britain have jobs today. Research has not yet established with certainty what the extent of child employment in Britain is. We would argue that this is in part because those few researchers who have dealt with the issue have done so as a secondary aspect of studies with other aims. It is not surprising, therefore, that little attention has been paid to the methodological problems involved. We propose to review some of those problems, consider the available research in the light of these problems and move tentatively towards a conclusion on the extent of child employment.

METHODOLOGICAL ISSUES

We shall take as our starting point the report by Davies (1972), which had been funded by the Department of Health and Social Security. It combined two sorts of evidence. First, information gathered from school pupils themselves by questionnaire, backed up where necessary with interviews. Second, information about those pupils from their teachers. It appears that Davies submitted a full statistical report to the DHSS but only a four-page summary was ever made public. Davies concerned himself in that report with two main types of issue: first, the extent and character of children's employment, and second, the relationship between that work and the child's schooling.

With respect to the amount of employment, Davies had to begin by confronting an obviously important question: what is child employment? Davies decided to distinguish between two categories of employment, which he labelled category A and category B. As illustrations of the two categories, he cited newspaper delivery, which he placed in category A as it involves assisting in a trade or occupation carried out for profit, and babysitting, which fell into category B because it was a personal service without financial gain to the employer. The reason for the distinction, according to Davies, was that category A jobs were the subject of local authority bylaws under the Children and Young Persons Act 1933, whereas category B jobs were not. However, Davies did acknowledge that the precise scope of this Act is uncertain and presents difficulties of interpretation. He also drew attention to the fact that the Education Act 1944 empowers local authorities to prohibit or restrict *any* kind of employment prejudicial to a child's health or education. Davies thus argued the need for a study such as this to include all regular jobs, paid or unpaid.

Although Davies's approach may seem admirably thorough, there are other definitional problems which he does not confront. First, he does not define 'regular' employment. Thus we do not know in what circumstances a job might be excluded on the grounds of being irregular. Second, by including *unpaid* work and by including work undertaken *within the family* there is a danger of producing a notion of child work too broad to be useful. When discussing employment, it is worth while distinguishing, for example, between a child who looks after a younger sibling regularly for no payment and a child who receives money for babysitting for someone to whom he or she had been introduced for this precise purpose. We would also suggest that unpaid work within the family is particularly difficult to study by questionnaire. By their very nature, questionnaires place a burden of interpretation on the respondent. (We return to this issue in Chapter 7.) On the face of it, a child who regularly receives payment for delivering milk or serving in a shop would have little difficulty in correctly reporting his or her 'work'. Household chores in the family home might be treated differently by different respondents. If this argument is accepted, Davies's category A data is likely to be more reliable than his category B. We will return to the issue of using questionnaires to collect information on work within the family in Chapter 7.

A further problem of definition concerns the period covered in the report. Children may move in and out of employment. They may follow different work patterns during school holidays from term time. It is not clear in Davies's report whether figures refer to the current circumstances when the questionnaires were administered, the term in which the questionnaires were administered, that term plus the previous holiday, or the child's whole life to date. The distinctions are important; in our own research (to which we shall return later), we have found that typically for every two respondents who happen to be working at the time of being surveyed, there will be another not currently working who has worked in the past.

In his survey, Davies included third- and fourth-year secondary pupils in schools in England and Wales. Although he does not explain why he chose these particular pupils for study, his description of his subject matter as 'the out-of-school employment of boys and girls in the 13 to 15 plus age group' allows us to make an informed guess. For children *under* 13 years of age, the law forbids employment for all but a very narrow range of jobs where the parents are also involved. Thus, Davies may have believed that in covering 13-year-olds he was including the onset of employment among children. Compulsory schooling ends at 16 years of age. Thus to have included older school pupils might have produced evidence which would be difficult to interpret, since those of the same age who have left school would be excluded from the population studied. This last point seems to us a sound one; the end of compulsory schooling marks a suitable spot at which to end the study of 'child' employment, as opposed to 'youth' or 'adult' employment. However, to exclude younger children, and not to distinguish between different ages limits the usefulness of the data. Subsequent studies (e.g. MacLennan et al., 1985; Balding, 1991; Lavalette et al., 1991) show that, despite the law, many children report starting work before the age of 13 years. Such studies also show that, throughout most of the secondary school years, there is a fairly steady rise in the number of children who have worked. Thus, in collecting data on children's employment, it is preferable to distinguish between pupils of different ages or school years. In order to compare data satisfactorily with other samples, one must be clear about the ages of the pupils in the samples.

The basic method for collecting data which Davies employed was the questionnaire. However he indicates that respondents were subsequently interviewed if their written responses 'were found on inspection to be incomplete, ambiguous or extraordinary'. We are not told what proportion of respondents were interviewed, however, the very fact that some interviews were deemed necessary is evidence that Davies was aware that the questionnaire has limitations for this type of research. The fact that replies might seem 'extraordinary' is obviously an indication that what the respondent writes may not correspond to reality. The responses may be an inaccurate guide to what has actually occurred. This may be due to limitations in the child's ability to remember or to a desire to mislead. For example, with respect to memory, a 14-year-old may provide inaccurate information about work undertaken at the age of 11 or 12. Equally, a child may attempt to conceal or minimize activities known to be illegal or subject to social disapproval.

Some of these objections to questionnaires may be trivial in practice. We do not know the extent to which replies may be misleading in any given case. In a rare attempt to study children at work by observational methods, Steinberg et al. (1982b) found little connection between observers' reports and the children's self-reports. That study dealt with the detailed character of jobs rather than the broader, and presumably easier, questions of whether an individual was at work and when. It is necessary, when employing questionnaires, to be aware of their drawbacks, and form some sort of reasoned judgement on the likely accuracy of different types of questions. This message is particularly important because, for pragmatic financial reasons, questionnaires have shown themselves to be a very attractive tool to researchers.

The practicalities of empirical research also have a significance for a further issue, namely the nature of the sample. Davies reports the number of respondents, divided by sex, and describes their age range and the spectrum of schools from which they were drawn. The schools were of different types and were distributed over 10 regions of England and Wales. Other than that, the report does not indicate how they were selected. In addition, Davies does not report one potentially crucial point, what proportion of the actual population of the schools and classes selected actually answered the questionnaires. Those who are omitted will presumably have been absent from school and absentees may well have different characteristics from those actually sampled. If, as is possible, a substantial commitment to work sometimes goes with a reduced commitment to schooling, the omission of absentees may lead to the amount of actual child employment being underestimated.

In summary, the main methodological issues for studying the extent of child employment which arise from this review of the Davies study are:

1. What activities are to be classified as 'work'?
2. What other aspects of the circumstances will be taken into account, e.g.
   a) Is payment received?
   b) Is the employer a parent or other close relative?
   c) Does the work take place in the home?
3. Is there a minimum duration before the activity counts as work?
4. Is the age at which the work is undertaken taken into account?
5. Is the representativeness of the sample established, particularly with reference to the proportion of the target population the sample forms?
6. What is the time gap between the activities on which the respondents are being questioned and the replies being made?
7. Is the pattern of schooling taken into account, e.g. by distinguishing between work on school days, work at weekends during school term, and work during school vacations?

Researchers setting out to discover how many children are working may very well get different answers depending on how they handle these issues. If the researchers state their position on each issue clearly, we can take that into account when interpreting their results. The greatest problems arise when researchers fail to state how they handled these problems.

Let us now consider the evidence on offer since Davies concerning the extent of child employment in Britain, bearing in mind these issues. Although, as we shall find, most studies have not taken a clear position on some of these variables, thus reducing the value of the evidence collected, nevertheless, some general indications of the extent of child employment may be obtained.

REVIEW OF EVIDENCE

Since Davies's study in 1972, there have been several empirically-based attempts to make estimates of the numbers of school children under the statutory school-leaving age who have jobs. These include nationwide surveys covering many thousands of respondents but also some much smaller scale investigations. Some of these are academic studies, some by campaigning organizations, some by journalists, one by a government research unit. In certain cases child labour was the sole or main focus of the research; in other cases it was more peripheral. We are not aware of having overlooked any large-scale study, but because we have been willing to include some very small-scale studies, some equally small ones may have escaped our notice.

In this section we have excluded studies of child labour which do not attempt a numerical estimate of its extent (e.g. Murray, 1991). We exclude studies which deal only with school pupils above minimum school-leaving age (e.g. Tymms and Fitz-Gibbon, 1992), unless they provide some retrospective data on the respondents' work history when younger (e.g. Hutson, 1990). We also initially exclude consideration of studies by the present authors but shall discuss that work later in the chapter. Only one study (Hibbett and Beatson, 1995) claims to be statistically representative of the country as a whole. However, several authors (e.g. Pond and Searle, 1991) discuss their own findings as if they could be treated as representative, for want of any better estimates.

By far the biggest studies in terms of sample size were those by Balding (1991, 1993, 1994) which covered over 19,000, over 20,000 and over 29,000 pupils respectively. However, employment was only one issue dealt within a more broadly based health-related questionnaire. Pupils were asked to answer about the current term. Unfortunately, despite the size of the samples, these studies turn out to be not particularly helpful guides to the extent of employment. Balding's sampling was not systematic, relying as he did on the voluntary cooperation of schools, and he varied the specific wording of the questions from year to year.

None of the other, smaller studies, taken in isolation, can claim to be representative of the population at large. Because child employment was frequently not the main focus of the study, systematic sampling often refers to some narrower population group, such as early school leavers. Smaller studies which are focused on child employment generally deal with pupils in a small range of schools, whose representativeness can only be judged impressionistically. Some of the smaller studies describe the sample surveyed, without discussing those members of the target population not covered. Thus they may suffer from the same bias towards underestimation which we suggested might have existed in the Davies study.

Three reports other than Balding's cover large numbers, the England and Wales Youth Cohort Study (Courtenay and McAleese, 1993, where there were 14,111 respondents), and two studies in Scotland (Main and Raffe, 1983, 2,620 respondents, and Howieson, 1990, 3,902 respondents). All three were based on postal surveys and were asking questions some time after the respondents had reached minimum school-leaving age. Questions on work while under the minimum school-leaving age were therefore being answered retrospectively and the problem of quality of recall arises. Courtenay and McAleese included a single question about part-time work in Years 10 and 11, which is thus not particularly informative for present purposes, since work in either year or in both years cannot be distinguished. The Scottish studies asked about 'jobs before leaving school', but since the respondents included pupils who left school beyond the minimum age, interpretation of the data presented difficulties, since 'jobs before leaving school' can include jobs both before and after the minimum leaving age had been attained. The study by Roberts et al. (1986, with 854 respondents) is also retrospective, but has the advantage of being based on interviews. Hutson (1990) surveyed 470 respondents aged 17 and 18 years old, so this, too, was a retrospective study as far as employment below age 16 was concerned.

There are two questionnaire studies by the Low Pay Unit, each of which involved substantial samples, MacLennan et al., 1985 (1,698 respondents) and Pond and Searle, 1991 (1,827 respondents). These studies were specifically focused on child employment as was the Young People at Work survey carried out by the Economics, Research and Education Division of the Department of Employment (Hibbett and Beatson, 1995). This was conducted by interview and covered a representative sample of 1,663 of 13- to 18-year-olds throughout the United Kingdom. Within the whole sample there were 772 falling into the age range 13 to 15 years.

No other study has a sample greater than 600. The biggest of these is by Lavalette (1994), who reports three studies which together cover 567 respondents. Other academic studies cover smaller samples: Finn, 1984 (147); Holmes and Croll, 1989 (79); Mizen, 1992 (152); Brown, 1987 (200); and Wallace, 1987 (153). Of these, the last two provide very vague information on employment. However, they are already cited in the literature (see, for example, Mizen, 1992) and, for that reason, are included.

The other studies are essentially journalistic reports with no claim to meet academic standards. However, each has something of interest in it. They are Spittles, 1973 (528 respondents); Combes, 1987 (no sample size stated); Notarangelo and Dutter, 1991 (280).

Let us consider first of all those studies which provide some information on the extent to which children *ever* work at all prior to reaching the minimum school-leaving age.

Table 2.1 summarizes the evidence. We have tried to indicate, where information was given, whether the particular researchers employed a broad or a narrow definition of employment, although in some cases the authors were silent on the matter of definition. By 'narrow' we mean a definition roughly equivalent to

TABLE 2.1 Percentage of children *ever* working prior to minimum school-leaving age.

Authors	Percentage	Definition[a]
1. *Retrospective studies*		
Roberts et al.	42	?
Hutson	65	?
2. *Studies near minimum school-leaving age*		
Brown	<50	?
Wallace	100	?
Finn	77	?
Mizen	69	?
Lavalette (study 2)	63	broad
Hibbett and Beatson	61	broad

[a] Definition: Do the authors give a broad or narrow definition. Where there is no discussion of definition, this is indicated by '?'.

Davies's category A; by 'broad' we mean a definition which would include both category A and category B.

Roberts and his colleagues interviewed 17- and 18-year-olds. Theirs is clearly the smallest of the seven estimates. The relatively low figure is probably associated with the fact that it is indeed a retrospective study. As noted above, Brown and Wallace report their findings very casually and their results should be treated with caution.

Hibbett and Beatson unfortunately do not appear to have asked whether the child had ever worked; they do report on whether the child had had a job in the past year. This almost certainly means that the figure included above underestimates the proportion of their sample who had ever worked.

The remaining four studies may be tentatively considered to give the best estimates. It is notable that they showed a degree of consensus, the estimates varying only between 63 per cent and 77 per cent. Such variations could easily be due to regional or other differences between the samples. Only Lavalette gives a clear indication of the definition being employed and it is noticeable that, although it is a broad definition, his percentage figure is the lowest of the four 'good' estimates.

Let us now look at children of different ages, starting with the oldest, those in their last year of compulsory schooling (see Table 2.2). Some research reports classify respondents by the stage of school they are at, in which case they will be in Year 11 or Fifth Form in England, S4 in Scotland. Where the sample is described by age rather than school stage, these respondents are 15 years old.

Main and Raffe asked about work undertaken in the last term before leaving school. Like Roberts et al., their sample contains some cases of later leavers.

Both MacLennan et al. and Balding report male and female results separately. However, whereas MacLennan et al. does so in a way which permits us to calculate a combined male–female score, Balding does not. As a very rough guide to an

TABLE 2.2 Working at age 15.

Authors	Percentages	Definition
1. *Retrospective studies*		
Main and Raffe	36	?
2. *Studies near minimum school-leaving age*		
MacLennan et al.	44	narrow
Balding 1991 (71 female, 60 male)	65.5[a]	broad
Balding 1993 (54 female, 47 male)	50.5[a]	broad
Lavalette (study 2)	37	broad
[b]Spittles	37	?
[b]Lavalette (study 3)	33	broad
Hibbett and Beatson	61	broad

[a] Median of female and male scores, since mean for all respondents was not reported. Individual male and female percentages are given in brackets.
[b] Includes some 14-year-old respondents.

overall figure for Balding's subjects we have taken the midpoint between the male and female percentages.

MacLennan et al. asked about current term-time working. Balding's question (1991) was:

Do you do a regular paid job during term time?

In 1993 it was:

Do you have a regular paid job outside school during term time?

This may be compared with Lavalette, who here is reporting those who say they are *currently* working, i.e. employed at the time of the study. Hibbett and Beatson, as we have already noted, report numbers who had worked in the past year, so in this context, the figure is probably an overestimate. Differences in wording might account for some of the differences between the findings. Balding may have obtained 'Yes' responses from those not actually working at the time of the study but who had done so earlier in the term.

The studies by Lavalette and by Spittles combine the 15-year-olds with 14-year-olds and hence are a less precise guide to 15-year-olds as a group. Even if we disregard Main and Raffe, Spittles, and Lavalette (study 3) as the least likely to be reliable, we are still left with wider variations than for estimates of how many *ever* work, the variations in estimates ranging between 37 per cent and 65.5 per cent.

Evidence about younger age groups or earlier school years is less common and we shall consider it together. Table 2.3 includes two journalistic studies, Notarangelo and Dutter, which gives reasonably clear information on methods and results, and Spittles, which is less informative. It may be significant that the former produces results in line with other studies whilst the latter does not.

As with older children, Lavalette's results are somewhat lower than for other studies, perhaps reflecting the region in which he collected the data.

The main sources for each age level are MacLennan et al. and Balding. Since Balding has the broader definition, it is not surprising that his figures are almost invariably larger. The discrepancy between the two sets of figures tends to fall as the children get younger with one striking exception, at age 11. It should be remembered that MacLennan et al.'s sample is confined to a narrower geographical range than Balding's. Even more significant, perhaps, is that at this age level, MacLennan et al. had only 94 respondents, 40 of them female, of whom 21 are classified as employed. Balding's sample sizes at this age level were much larger (e.g. for 1991, 1224). We are thus inclined to treat MacLennan et al.'s data in this case as a less useful guide.

Our tentative conclusions on the 'best estimates' available are summarized in Table 2.4. Stressing, once again, the highly tentative nature of the judgements which led to this summary, let us ask ourselves whether the picture which emerges from it makes sense.

It would appear that older children are more likely to be working than younger, which might fit commonsense expectations. On the other hand there is only a

TABLE 2.3 Working at earlier ages.

Authors	Percentages	Definition
1. *Age 14/ English Year 10/Scottish S3*		
MacLennan et al.	40	narrow
Balding 1991 (57 female, 61 male)	59[a]	broad
Balding 1992 (41 female, 44 male)	42.5[a]	broad
Balding 1993 (40 female, 42 male)	41[a]	broad
Notarangelo and Dutter	51	?
Lavalette (study 1)	36	broad
Hibbett and Beatson	51	broad
2. *Age 13/English Year 2/Scottish S2*		
MacLennan et al.	38	narrow
Combes	75	?
Balding 1991 (44 female, 54 male)	49[a]	broad
Balding 1992 (32 female, 36 male)	34[a]	broad
Balding 1993 (31 female, 37 male)	34[a]	broad
Hibbett and Beatson	42	broad
3. *Age 12/English Year 1/Scottish S1*		
MacLennan et al.	33	narrow
Balding 1991 (30 female, 43 male)	36.5[a]	broad
Balding 1992 (20 female, 29 male)	24.5[a]	broad
Balding 1993 (21 female, 24 male)	22.5[a]	broad
4. *Age 11/English Year 7/Scottish P7*		
MacLennan et al.	44	narrow
Balding 1991 (23 female, 29 male)	26[a]	broad
Balding 1992 (11 female, 19 male)	15[a]	broad
Balding 1993 (16 female, 22 male)	19[a]	broad

[a] Median of female and male scores, percentage for male and female samples are in brackets.

TABLE 2.4 Best estimates of children working.

1. Percentages who have *ever* worked before leaving school	63–77
2. Percentages working at age 15	36–66
3. Percentages working at age 14	36–59
4. Percentages working at age 13	34–49
5. Percentages working at age 12	22.5–36.5
6. Percentages working at age 11	15–26

slight indication in the figures above that 15-year-olds work more than 14-year-olds. This may be due to the fact that as children approach formal public examinations some of them give up work to concentrate on schooling. This is consistent with the estimates of 'ever worked' being greater than estimates of 15-year-olds working. It might also account for the greater variations in estimates at 15 than for younger children, in that different studies may be answered by children who happen to be at different points in their choices about work versus school. It may also be that there are regional or class differences in response to such decisions.

We have not so far cited in these discussions about the extent of child employment the study by Pond and Searle mentioned in the introduction. The value of their extensive study is some what reduced by the fact that they include children between 10 and 16 (predominantly between 11 and 15) *and do not distinguish between them in terms of age or stage of schooling*. Since, as we have seen, there are strong indications that more 15-year-olds work than 11-year-olds, it is difficult to compare their data with other studies which deal with narrower age bands or report different age bands separately. They report 32 per cent working during term; when those who worked in the previous holiday are included the figure rises to 43 per cent. Their definition of work was narrow. These figures are quite compatible with the estimates we have made above.

RESEARCH BY THE PRESENT AUTHORS

We have recently undertaken, in five areas of south-west Scotland and northern England, studies of the extent, nature and effects of child employment. The areas were not chosen as representative of Britain as a whole, since in four cases we were commissioned to undertake local studies. However, the data collected in these studies on the extent of work among school-aged children forms a useful complement to the earlier studies we have been reviewing. (Some of this evidence has appeared previously in reports on individual regional surveys, e.g. Hobbs et al., 1993b; Lavalette et al., 1996; McKechnie et al., 1993; McKechnie et al., 1994.)

Aware of the difficulties which have arisen in trying to interpret studies which have employed differently phrased questions and employed different criteria (or unspecified criteria) for defining work, we decided to follow Lavalette's approach, which seemed to us the most satisfactory so far. We posed a series of questions designed to establish how many of the respondents were *currently working* at the time of the survey and how many had *ever worked*. These questions were asked directly but answers were interpreted in the light of supplementary questions about the character of the work. We included as 'work' any sort of paid employment or activity for gain, other than that undertaken within the immediate family. Our results are directly comparable with those of Lavalette already cited. They are also comparable with the other studies cited, provided due attention is paid to the differences in research procedures we have already discussed.

Our studies have concentrated on the older age groups. Data is collected on what work they are currently, or have recently, participated in. This reduces the time gap between the event and recall reducing the risk of false recall. We have also asked questions about past employment, and in that sense do rely on some retrospective recall. In Scotland we have covered 606 pupils in S4 (around 15 years of age) in two urban schools and three rural. In England, one study dealt with 281 Year 11 pupils in two urban schools, another with 490 Year 10 pupils in three urban and one rural schools, a third dealt with 488 Year 10 pupils and 366 Year 11 pupils in three urban schools. To avoid problems of sub-sampling in each study the full year cohort was the intended sample. The results are summarized in Tables 2.5 to 2.7.

TABLE 2.5 Percentages ever worked and currently working: Scotland S4.

School	Type[a]	N[b]	Current	Ever
Scottish 1	U	194	36	65
Scottish 2	U	153	35	61
Scottish 3	R	80	36	75
Scottish 4	R	71	32	66
Scottish 5	R	108	35	69
TOTAL		606	35	67

[a] R: rural; U: urban.
[b] N: number of students in each category.

TABLE 2.6 Percentages ever worked and currently working: England Year 10.

School	Type[a]	N[b]	Current	Ever
English 1	U	154	41	66
English 2	R	108	75	88
English 3	U	50	70	90
English 4	U	178	38	65
English 7	U	141	25	38
English 8	U	181	27	44
English 9	U	146	49	71
TOTAL		958	49	69

[a] R: rural; U: urban.
[b] N: number of students in each category.

TABLE 2.7 Percentages ever worked and currently working: England Year 11.

School	Type[a]	N[b]	Current	Ever
English 5	U	222	49	76
English 6	U	59	36	88
English 7	U	101	21	37
English 8	U	121	31	49
English 9	U	144	34	56
TOTAL		647	37	62

[a] R: rural; U: urban.
[b] N: number of students in each category.

The Scottish data is most directly comparable with Lavalette's study 2 which was also of S4 pupils. Our figures for currently working (35 per cent) and ever worked (67 per cent) are very similar to his (37 per cent and 63 per cent respectively). Lavalette's figures tended to be rather lower than some other studies and this may now be regarded as at least in part due to differences between Scotland and England.

The Year 10 figures (Table 2.6) are relatively higher than those obtained in Scotland. The Year 11 figures (Table 2.7) are rather closer to the Scottish results. However, more important may be the fact that there is a great deal more variation from school to school than in Scotland. Scottish schools' 'Current Workers' varied only between 32 and 36 per cent. The equivalent range for Year 10 of the English schools is 25 to 75 per cent. In Year 11, the English range is not quite so large, 21 to 49 per cent, but it is still comparatively broad compared with the Scottish figures. The inter-school variation in Scotland in the percentages who have ever worked is 61 to 75 per cent. In England the equivalent ranges are 38 to 90 per cent (Year 10) and 36 to 88 per cent (Year 11).

Such variations may be due to differences in the economic and social settings of the respective schools. The main lesson to be learnt is that since schools can differ considerably in the amount of experience of work their pupils have had, the same may hold true of regions. Seeing this, we can account for at least some of the variations between the findings of other studies, most of which were based on particular regions and particular schools. Our total sample in the English and Scottish schools consisted of 2,131 pupils. The results emerging of 40 per cent currently employed and 66 per cent ever employed cannot be regarded as precisely indicating the national picture, given that they were confined to four regions and we have discovered regional variations. On the other hand, as Table 2.8 indicates, they are entirely consistent with the estimates we made on the basis of our review of past research.

TABLE 2.8 Comparison of percentages.

	Estimates from past research	Present results
Ever worked	63–77	66
Working at age 15	37–66[a]	36 currently working
Working at age 14	34[a]–59[a]	49 currently working

[a] Median of male and female scores.

CONCLUSIONS

We do not claim that we have produced a precise figure for the percentage of school-aged children working in Britain today. What we believe we have done, however, is to establish that there is overwhelming evidence that *employment is a majority experience* for these children. The research indicates that most children will have had at least one job before they reach school-leaving age. The onus is on anyone who wishes to suggest that child employment in Britain is trivial or marginal to present relevant evidence that this is the case.

As was noted in the introduction to this chapter, a government spokesperson was dismissive of an estimate by the London Low Pay Unit of the number of school children currently working in Britain (Pond and Searle, 1991). Let us consider the argument in the light of the studies we have been reviewing. The Low Pay Unit case is stated thus:

> We have shown that more than 40 per cent of children have some form of employment ... There are about 4 million children of secondary school age in Britain. If applied to the country as a whole, our results would suggest that 1.75 to 2 million of those are working. (Pond and Searle, 1991, p. 15.)

By the phrase 'children of secondary school age' they presumably meant between 11 and 15 years old, the ages of the vast majority of children in their own study. Based on their finding of 43 per cent of children with a job, one may make an extrapolation to the whole country of only around 1.72 million, slightly lower than the figures Pond and Searle offer.

The most recently published government figures indicate the 11–15-year-old population to be marginally over 3.5 million (Central Statistical Office, 1994). Using the best estimates of current employment from the studies we have been considering, this would suggest that at any given time between 1.1 and 1.7 million of this age range might be working. However, remembering that children move in and out of employment, it might be better to consider how many children will have worked at some time before the statutory minimum school-leaving age. The studies we reviewed would indicate a figure between 2.2 and 2.6 million. Our own research suggests a figure of around 2.3 million.

At the time of the government's dismissal of Pond and Searle's estimate, there were no publicly available official statistics on child employment. As we have seen, the results of a government-sponsored survey did subsequently appear. Hibbett and Beatson (1995) claim that theirs was the 'first comprehensive nationwide' survey for over twenty years, presumably referring back to the study by Davies (1972) we considered earlier. Hibbett and Beatson also refer to Pond and Searle's study as 'of limited value' since they cover 'just a single local labour market'. It seems appropriate then to consider the extent of the similarities and differences in the Low Pay Unit and the Department of Employment studies. Although they themselves do not publish the calculation, it is easy to derive from Hibbett and Beatson's figures an estimate of the child labour force in Britain. This can be done by using, on the one hand, their estimated national population of the 13 to 15 age group, and on the other hand, the percentages of 13-, 14- and 15-year-olds in their sample who have worked in the past year. The outcome is a figure of just over 1.0 million. This is a good deal lower than Pond and Searle's estimate (1.75 to 2.0) million. However, unlike Pond and Searle, Hibbett and Beatson do not include 11- and 12-year-olds. For 13-, 14- and 15-year-olds, we found Hibbett and Beatson's findings not dissimilar to other studies, including our own. It seems reasonable, therefore, to take account of studies which do consider 11- and 12-year-olds separately to provide an estimated figure which could be added to Hibbett and Beatson's. Our 'best estimates' in Table 2.5 suggested that around 29.5 per cent of 12-year-olds and around 20.5 per cent of 11-year-olds have jobs. Given that there are around 1.5 million children of this age in Britain, one could estimate that around 350,000 to 400,000 of them might have a job. Adding them to Hibbett and Beatson's figure, we find an estimate of 1.4 million 11- to 15-year-olds work. This is a good deal closer to Pond and Searle's figure (and of course in line with our estimates of 1.1 to 1.7 million).

Looked at in that light, the Low Pay Unit estimate does not seem to be so misleading after all. The government's rejection of their figures does not seem justified, in the light of other studies, and, in particular, in the light of the findings of a survey by a government department.

Chapter 3

The Nature of Children's Jobs

INTRODUCTION

The previous chapter focused upon estimating the extent of child employment in Britain. We showed with reasonable certainty that most children in Britain appear to have had some sort of experience of the world of work by the time they reach the age of 16, the earliest time at which they can legally leave school. However, we also noted that different researchers have meant different things when they refer to children having jobs.

In this chapter, we move from considering how many children have jobs to looking more closely at what these jobs are. We shall review the results of studies carried out by the present authors in five different areas of Scotland and England. Broadly similar questions were posed to the pupils in all five areas and the same methodological assumptions were made in each case. Thus the results from the different areas can be compared with some confidence. In addition, where it proves practical, the results from the present studies will be compared with other research.

We shall start by refreshing our memories about the levels of employment that were found. We shall now identify more clearly some of the regions in which these studies were carried out. All of the subjects were between the ages of 14 and 15 years and were in the last two years of compulsory schooling (in Scotland this equates with S3 and S4, in England Year 10 and Year 11). Table 3.1 indicates the

Table 3.1 Extent of work experience: percentages.

	Current worker	Former worker	Never worker	N[b]
Urban Scottish[a]	32	29	36	347
Dumfries and Galloway	35	36	30	259
Cumbria	50	22	27	490
North Tyneside	46	38	21	281
Blackburn	32	18	50	854

[a] Specific location withheld at request of local education authority.
[b] N: number of students in each category.

areas and the percentages of the respondents who were current workers, former workers and who had never worked.

A consideration of Table 3.1 shows not only that it is common for school pupils to work but that there are some regional variations. Indeed, as was shown in the previous chapter, variations between schools within the same region can be found. In Cumbria, for example, the percentage of children currently working varied from 39 per cent in one school to 75 per cent in another. One possible explanation is that the level of employment reflects the specific economic conditions of the area. For example, the highest level of current employment was recorded in an area where tourism is the major industry.

Some of the schools in Blackburn serve relatively deprived catchment areas. However, the extent of parental choice of school makes it difficult to draw too close comparisons between work and economic factors in the locality in that case. The findings may support the hypothesis of children as a 'reserve army of labour' (see Lavalette, 1994; Lavalette et al., 1991). The buoyancy of the local economy is such that it highlights the shortage of the local labour supply and children are drawn into the workforce as substitutes for adults. This interpretation may have some truth to it but it could not account for all child employment. Why in areas which are less economically healthy do significant numbers of children still work? Is it because of economic necessity?

In North Tyneside we obtained evidence of the social composition of the school populations in terms of the level of free school meals and clothing grants. In one school, which we shall call Brickhall, there was a far higher incidence of free school meals and clothing grants indicating a lower socio-economic catchment group. Yet the extent of working in the two schools was very similar, Actonvale having 36 per cent current workers and 30 per cent former workers, whereas for Brickhall the figures were 35 per cent and 28 per cent respectively.

Such a finding hardly supports the 'economic necessity' argument. There may be other reasons for such patterns of employment and simplistic stereotyped views will not provide a sufficient explanation of child employment.

For the time being then we have to withhold judgement on why children work in Britain today. Irrespective of the reasons for children working, it must be acknowledged that they are participants in the world of work. If this is the case, then what is the nature of their employment experience?

NATURE OF EMPLOYMENT

The common stereotype which exists in Britain is that children who work are employed in newspaper delivery. Our society has constructed a notion that certain types of work can be viewed as 'children's jobs', where the aim is to acquire 'extra pocket money'. As we saw in Chapter 1, such a stereotype was conjured up by government ministers arguing against a recent European Community directive on child employment. But is this view of the nature of children's jobs justified?

In the studies being considered in this chapter, participants were asked not only if they had jobs but what type of jobs they were doing. Table 3.2 shows the distribution of jobs for the five areas.

Table 3.2 shows that the dominant category of employment is in fact delivery work. This includes newspaper delivery, morning and evening, and milk delivery. The latter can involve very early morning starts with 4.00 a.m. not being uncommon. However, less than half of the jobs are of the delivery sort. Children are employed in a wide range of other activities including shop work, hotel and catering and waiting. We might be more likely to think of these jobs as 'adult' rather than 'children's jobs'. A smaller percentage of children were working in hawking (door-to-door selling, which included a range of products from cosmetics to confectionery). Within the 'other' category we found small numbers of children employed in a range of jobs, including packing, gardening, work in garages and building sites, cleaning, modelling and working in a sawmill.

A substantial number of children were employed in babysitting. Indeed in North Tyneside it was reported more frequently than delivery work and in Blackburn it was about as common as delivery work. It is not clear why there should be such high levels of babysitting in these English urban areas. It might be due to social attitudes, such as notions of how young a 'babysitter' may be acceptable. Alternatively, it might be related to differences in the leisure or work patterns of adults. Unfortunately, our research provided us with no evidence to follow the issue of 'why' any further.

Researchers have varied in their treatment of this form of employment. Pond and Searle (1991) excluded babysitting from their study, arguing that it was not prohibited by bylaws or national legislation. Others, such as Hibbett and Beatson (1995), have argued that it should be included in any study of employment since it is a common form of female employment. Exclusion would misrepresent the

TABLE 3.2 Main types of jobs.

| | Scotland | | | England | |
	Urban	Rural[a]	Cumbria	N. Tyneside	Blackburn
Delivery	40	24	25	26	27
Hawking	3	1	4	5	4
Shop work	37	16	17	12	13
Babysitting	5	18	17	38	27
Waiting	7	17	7	2	3
Farm work	0	4	0	1	0
Hotel and Catering	0	8	20	8	9
Other	12	12	10	9	17

[a] Dumfries and Galloway.

gender divide in child employment. In this set of studies babysitting has been included because many children perceived it as their form of paid employment and because it involves a financial arrangement with members outside the family. In addition, the degree of responsibility placed on young people who are caring for younger children is perhaps an issue that deserves attention.

Geographical and economic variation appears to result in differences in the employment profiles across the studies. In the case of the Cumbrian data, a large percentage of those working were employed in the hotel and catering and shop-work sectors. This partly reflects the tourist-based economies which are to be found in some parts of this county.

The urban Scottish sample is dominated by delivery work, reflecting the urban base needed for such employment to flourish. In areas such as Dumfries and Galloway and Cumbria, where large concentrations of housing are rarer, this form of employment is less common.

In all of the regions the percentage recording farm work as their paid employment is very low. The highest figure (only 4 per cent) was recorded in the most rural area in these studies, Dumfries and Galloway. However, it should be remembered that we are dealing here with work outside the family. We have no evidence of how many children work on their own family's farm. It is particularly important not to overlook this possibility because there is another sort of evidence suggesting the importance of child labour on the farm. Cameron, Bishop and Sibert (1992) record a number of accidents involving children on farms. The research indicates that farm-related accidents peak at certain ages. One such peak occurs at around 14 years of age and the indications are that the children involved are often working on the farm when the accidents occur. As a result of using farm equipment, they end up as an accident statistic.

Our definition of 'work' may underestimate the extent of children working, not only on farms but also in other family enterprises such as shops. In Blackburn, at the request of the local authority sponsoring the research, we included questions about paid work at home and paid work for the family outside the home. Around 14 per cent of pupils had occasionally done paid work at home and another 2 per cent had done so 'frequently'. Rather more said they had undertaken paid work outside the home for the parents, 19 per cent occasionally and 7 per cent frequently. This compares with the finding of Hibbett and Beatson (1995) that 6 per cent of 13- to 15-year-olds who had not had any paid work outside the family had had paid work within the family in the year leading up to the survey. We feel such figures should be treated with caution, for the reasons we explained in Chapter 1. The relationship of home work, work in the family business, pocket money and payment may be a complex one. Answers to questions which must of necessity be phrased in a simple way do not necessarily accurately represent the complex reality.

Consideration of the types of jobs done by children must lead us to challenge the traditional image of 'children's jobs' and acknowledge that such a stereotype misrepresents the reality of children's experience. The data clearly shows children working in a range of jobs, many of which are more likely to be perceived as adult forms of employment. Lavalette et al. (1995) suggest that, in these latter areas, children may be in competition with adults in the labour market.

It would appear, however, that children do not enter straight into 'adult' forms of work. The study by Lavalette et al. (1995) shows that younger children are more likely to be employed in delivery work while older children are working in shops and waiting jobs. It is possible to speculate that the different forms of work have different status implications for children. From the studies we have carried out, many children, employed or thinking about seeking a job, aspire towards shopwork, particularly among the females. This suggests that research into the participants' perception of work may provide some valuable insights into the work experience of children. Unfortunately few studies have attempted to adopt such a methodology. One exception is a recent paper by McKechnie et al. (1996) where an interview strategy was employed to explore specific aspects of the work experience. Discussion of the results of this study will be considered in Chapter 6.

How representative are the conclusions on the types of jobs done by children which emerge from these studies? In turning to other research evidence, one problem arises from the fact that what limited British research there is spans two decades. Comparing the experience of employment between the earliest and the most recent studies may present problems. We must be cautious in assuming the population researched in the 1970s or early 1980s faced a similar environment to the one of the 1990s. It may be the case that the forms of employment have changed over time. For example, video hire shops did not exist in the 1970s but do now. Similarly there are more single-parent families in the 1990s than there were in the 1970s and this could be relevant when looking particularly at babysitting jobs.

To avoid this problem we have focused upon other studies published in the 1990s. Given that these studies were carried out over a similar time frame to our own, comparison between the studies should give us some insight into the representativeness of our conclusions. On occasion we will draw on the earlier research where data on a particular issue is limited.

Studies by Pond and Searle (1991), Mizen (1992), Balding (1993), Lavalette (1994), Hibbett and Beatson (1995) and Jolliffe et al. (1995) have all produced data on the types of jobs being done by children. We have re-analysed their data and categorized it according to our job types. While we acknowledge that variations in definition and classification makes this a dubious task, we believe that it is worth looking to see whether there are any obvious discrepancies among these studies or between our studies and theirs. Table 3.3 demonstrates the extent to which some consistency emerges from all of these studies.

From Table 3.3 it is possible to sustain our argument that children in our studies were found to be working in a wide range of jobs, many of them outside

TABLE 3.3 Job categories: percentages.

	A	B	C	D	E
Delivery	34	33	35	54	29
Hawking	1	4	–	5	2
Shop work	21	15	14	20	15
Babysitting	–	12	17	4	–
Waiting	–	–	–	12	–
Farm work	–	–	6	1	1
Hotel and Catering	10	12	12	–	4
Other	33	25	15	4	50

Study A Pond and Searle   B Mizen
       C Balding   D Lavalette
       E Jolliffe

of our conception of 'children's jobs'. Across all of these studies children are found working in shops, hotel, catering and so on. It could be argued that Table 3.3 actually obscures the diversity of tasks carried out by children for money.

The 'other' category in Table 3.3 is quite large for some of the studies. This simply reflects the fact that children were employed in jobs which did not figure in our original classification. In Jolliffe et al.'s study (1995), the 'other' category includes those found working in garages, on street markets, as furniture removers, on building sites, as cleaners and those involved in modelling or acting. Such examples are not unique to this study and reinforces the range of jobs that children do. In Hibbett and Beatson's study, occupational categories used for adult employment were applied, with the result that 73 per cent of jobs were categorized as 'other'. This is clearly of very limited descriptive value. It also made it inappropriate to try to convert Hibbett and Beatson's data into the categories employed in Table 3.3.

From these studies it can be argued that our results on the types of work carried out by children is not atypical. This conclusion has a general relevance to understanding child employment across Britain, since the other studies were carried out in different parts of country. These include Birmingham, Coventry, Clydeside and Greenwich.

HOURS WORKED

School pupils spend on average 28 hours per week at school. When you then consider the amount of time that can be spent in paid employment this could result in little time being left for leisure interests and homework, or what Greenberger and Steinberg (1986) refer to as 'time for exploration'.

Table 3.4 indicates the number of hours worked by those children in employment. If we average the number of hours worked, we find figures around

TABLE 3.4 Hours worked per week: percentages.

	Up to 5 hours	6 to 10 hours	10 hours and over
Urban Scottish	48	31	21
Dumfries and Galloway	31	46	24
Cumbria	42	38	17
North Tyneside	36	41	22
Blackburn	46	37	16

eight hours per week. However, that does not provide a great deal of insight into patterns of working since children do vary in the amount of time they devote to paid employment. Accordingly, the table categorizes the workers, differentiating between those working up to 5 hours per week, those working up to 10 hours per week, and those working over 10 hours per week.

The great majority of working children spend less than 10 hours per week at work. There are of course some regional variations. In the Urban Scottish sample almost half of those working (48 per cent) work for less than five hours per week while in Dumfries and Galloway only 31 per cent do so. These variations may in turn reflect the variation in dominant job types in each region. Approximately a fifth of those working were committing in excess of 10 hours per week to their part-time employment. This pattern was fairly consistent across the regions, percentages varying only between 17 per cent (Cumbria) and 24 per cent (Dumfries and Galloway). It should be noted too that in a few cases children reported working a great deal more than 10 hours per week.

Why consider the number of hours worked and when those hours are worked? One reason is the possibility that longer working hours may have a detrimental effect on school performance. We shall deal with that issue in Chapter 5.

Comparing our results with findings from other studies is problematic due to the variations in the categories used. MacLennan et al. (1985) noted that in their early 1980s study the majority of children worked for 10 hours or less per week. However they do draw attention to the fact that a large percentage did work in excess of 11 hours per week. In their London sample 21 per cent of females and 34 per cent of males worked 11 hours or more per week while the comparable figures for the Luton and Bedford sample were 21 per cent and 20 per cent for females and males, respectively. Mizen (1992) found that the average number of hours worked per week in his sample was 7 hours, with 29 per cent working more than 8 hours per week. Hibbett and Beatson (1995) found that 51 per cent of their 13- to 15-year-old sample worked up to five hours per week, 33 per cent worked between 6 and 12 hours, 16 per cent over 12 hours.

Lavalette (1994) and Balding (1993) provide a breakdown of the numbers of hours worked which allows a direct comparison with our data. In the case of Balding we have focused on the 14–15-year sample since this is most directly comparable with our own age groups.

TABLE 3.5 Hours worked per week in other studies: percentages.

	Up to 5 hours	6 to 10 hours	10 hours and over	N[a]
Balding	47	37	16	3401
Lavalette:				
Study 1	41	32	27	75
Study 2	33	38	29	55
Study 3a	52	26	23	31
Study 3b	48	26	26	23

[a] N: number of students in each category.

As with all 'averaging' processes we do lose some feel for the range of hours worked. At the lower end this might be that some children work for only an hour a week on top of their school week. However every study that has attended to the number of hours has shown that some children commit a large number of hours to their work. For example Mizen noted one child working 28 hours per week. In our own studies we have also found examples of pupils working a large number of hours per week.

The comparison suggests some degree of consistency in the finding across all these studies. Whilst the majority work less than 10 hours per week, there is a large enough percentage of children working in excess of 10 hours per week to warrant concern, particularly when we bear in mind that these are full-time school pupils.

Looking at the number of hours children work gives us only a very general indication of the role this must play in their lives. It is also relevant to consider when these hours are worked. Table 3.6 shows the number of children who start work before 7.00 a.m. and the percentage who finish after 7.00 p.m. These start and finish times have not been chosen at random. The 1933 Children and Young Persons Act and the equivalent 1937 Act for Scotland specify that children are prohibited from working before 7.00 a.m. and after 7.00 p.m.

Given the other restrictions on the hours a child may work, stopping and starting times reported do not usually refer to the same job. They should be taken as indicating when in the day a particular job is undertaken. The most obvious 'time-linked' activities are milk and newspaper delivery. The former is almost always an early morning task. The same applies to newspaper delivery other than

TABLE 3.6 Start and finish times: percentages.

	Start before 7.00 a.m.	Finish after 7.00 p.m.
Urban Scottish	33	51
Dumfries and Galloway	29	63
Cumbria	28	51
North Tyneside	34	60
Blackburn	43	42

evening newspapers. On the whole, milk delivery is associated with the earliest starts.

Table 3.6 indicates that significant numbers of working children are employed outside of these watersheds. The issue of the legality of child employment will be returned to later in this chapter. For the present we need to note that many children rise very early on schooldays to work before going to school and significant numbers of them work late into the evening.

There are some local variations in starting and stopping times and it may be argued that it reflects different types of jobs typically undertaken in certain schools. Schools in Cumbria illustrate this point clearly (see Table 3.7).

TABLE 3.7   Cumbrian start and finish times: percentages.

School	Start before 7.00 a.m.	Finish after 7.00 p.m.
A	46	39
B	9	67
C	22	50
D	33	45

In schools A and D, in Table 3.7, where delivery work accounted for the majority of jobs we find the highest percentage of pupils working before 7.00 a.m., 46 per cent and 33 per cent respectively. Conversely, where babysitting and hotel and catering work accounted for a high proportion of working pupils (school B), we find a higher number of workers finishing work after the 7.00 p.m. watershed.

Few other studies provide much information on starting and finishing times. Pond and Searle (1991) note that working before 7.00 a.m. or after 7.00 p.m. contributed to a percentage of the pupils in their studies being categorized as working illegally but fail to provide a breakdown of this data. Lavalette (1994) is the only other researcher who attends to this important variable in his research. Across his three studies he found that a large percentage was working before 7.00 a.m. (study 1: 23 per cent; study 2: 44 per cent; study 3: 34 per cent). Similarly a large percentage of pupils were working beyond the 7.00 p.m. watershed (study 1: 69 per cent; study 2: 40 per cent; study 3: 54 per cent). Such findings reinforce the results from our own studies and indicate the extent to which the legislation regarding starting and finishing times are breached.

EARNINGS

How well are children rewarded for this work? One of the potential problems that arises in considering this question is the way we conceptualize the reward for work. For many, such as the government ministers cited previously, child employment is undertaken for 'pocket money'. Others assume that children work at least in part because of their family's poverty. Yet another view is that children feel the need to work to fulfil the 'needs' created by a consumer society. Whichever view is correct, and they may all contain some element of truth, it is worth trying to establish just how much children do actually earn.

Table 3.8 indicates the average hourly rate and average weekly rate for each of our studies.

TABLE 3.8 Hourly and weekly earnings: averages.

	Per hour	Per week
Urban Scottish	£2.34	£13.97
Dumfries and Galloway	£1.79	£12.99
Cumbria	£2.11	£13.80
North Tyneside	£1.80	£11.85

TABLE 3.9 Hourly earnings: percentages.

	Up to £1.00	£1.01 to £2.00	£2.01 to £3.00	Over £3.00
Urban Scottish	16	62	7	15
Dumfries and Galloway	8	73	15	4
Cumbria	13	42	32	10
North Tyneside	25	45	19	10

Let us consider some evidence on earnings collected by other researchers. Jolliffe et al. (1995) have analysed their data in terms of weekly wage rates and the percentage of those children working that fall into each category. They found that 45 per cent of working children were earning less than £10.00 per week and that 78 per cent earned less than £20.00 per week. There is no information supplied on the number of hours worked in a week.

Other studies such as MacLennan et al. (1985) do provide more specific information on hourly and weekly pay rates but the data was collected a decade ago and comparison with the present data set is complicated by inflation. Even the data we have collected in our own studies is spread over several years in the 1990s. It should be noted that we have not included the Blackburn data in these earnings tables. However, since in Blackburn evidence was collected from children of different ages, we shall consider those findings later.

Pond and Searle (1991) do not provide any information on the average weekly income for their sample. However, they found that the average hourly rate of pay in their study was £1.80. The majority of the employed children, 52 per cent, were earning £2.00 or less per hour. In addition they remind us of the dangers of dealing with 'average' income, namely that it can conceal the marked variation that can exist around the mean value. They report that a small percentage, 7 per cent, of the children in their sample were earning 50 pence or less per hour. At the other extreme they found one instance of a child earning £8.33 per hour. We have also found this wide variation in pay rates in our research. The lowest hourly pay rate we recorded was 10 pence per hour.

Mizen (1992) found the average hourly and weekly rates of pay were £1.60 and £13.70, respectively. This hourly rate is lower than any of the hourly rates found in any of our studies. However, he also found that the average weekly earnings lie within the range of weekly pay rates that were found in our studies. The implication would be that the children in Mizen's study would have to work longer hours to reach this weekly pay rate than children in our studies.

Balding (1993) provides the clearest breakdown of weekly earnings and, since he also provides the average hours worked, it is possible to calculate the hourly rate of pay for his sample. The data in Balding's study is broken down by age and sex and we have followed this format in Table 3.10.

TABLE 3.10 Hourly earnings by age: averages.

		Age:	11–12	12–13	13–14	14–15
Balding	Males		£1.69	£1.54	£1.79	£2.04
	Females		£1.07	£1.59	£1.78	£1.93
		Year:	7	8	9	10	11
Blackburn			£1.79	£1.55	£1.96	£2.01	£2.41

At first sight, comparisons made in Table 3.10 may not seem particularly fruitful. Balding provides data on males and females separately but not combined. One study discriminates on grounds of age, the other by school year. There was a gap of around four years between the collection of the two sets of data. However, despite these limitations, we may note that both show a general tendency for rates to rise with age (which might be expected) but both also show a slight dip in rates from 12 to 13 years and Year 8 (which we would not have predicted).

Within the limited range of studies available it is possible to argue that our results are in line with other research findings. From this area of investigation two questions emerge. First, against what standards do we judge the levels of pay that children receive? Second, what happens to this income? Some writers have argued that we should not underestimate the importance of this form of income, 'High levels of unemployment mean that a child may be the only breadwinner in the family' (Head, 1988: 20). Mizen (1992) also believes that where families are on low incomes the money from a child's job could be viewed as an important contribution. MacLennan et al. (1985) report two cases in their study where children indicated that they passed their income on to their family. More recently, Jolliffe et al. (1995) make reference to children passing their income on to their family.

While we do not deny that such cases exist there has been no systematic study of the role of children's income within the family context. That there is the need for such research is self-evident. Until it is possible to evaluate the contribution of the child's income to the family we will be left with individuals' opinions. As we have already argued it is simplistic to assume that poverty drives children to work. Financial hardship no doubt plays a part in understanding this phenomenon but it is not the whole story. In the United States researchers have concluded that it is the relatively well-off middle-class children who are more likely to work (Greenberger and Steinberg, 1986).

In one of our studies we carried out interviews with a number of working pupils (McKechnie et al., 1996). Part of the interview was related to the disposal of earned income. This was a relatively small-scale exercise and conclusions drawn must be tentative, but it does suggest hypotheses for other studies to investigate.

For example it appears that most children spent their income on 'consumables' such as clothes, compact discs, computer games and magazines. This conclusion is supported by Balding (1993), although he made no attempt to distinguish between the source of this money, i.e. pocket money given by parents or child's own earned income. Occasionally there was some reference made to saving a part of their income for holidays or because their parents wished it. If this turned out to be representative of the larger population of working children then the main contribution to family income arising from child employment would be a form of 'substitution', where the child's earning replaces family expenditure and reduces the burden on family resources, for example by removing the need for 'pocket money'.

Further research is needed in this area to test such hypotheses and to clarify the debate about the relationship between poverty and child employment.

GENDER DIFFERENCES

We have argued that the subtleties of the child labour market are only beginning to be realized. Part of this realization involves us in having to consider the sexual divide in child employment.

There is a long history of research concerned with the differences between adult male and female employment drawing attention to the gender divide. Studies of children's roles within the domestic environment have also highlighted the way in which children's roles within the home differ depending on their sex. Such studies focus upon their contribution to housework, the adults' perception of what are appropriate demands and the way they reflect differential treatment (Goodnow, 1988).

In this context, it is not unreasonable to expect some sort of gender divide in children's part-time paid employment. Let us begin by looking at the level of involvement in part-time work. Table 3.11 provides a breakdown of the number of males and females involved in the studies.

TABLE 3.11 Male and female participation.

	Male (%)	Female (%)	N[a]
Urban Scottish	47	53	347
Dumfries and Galloway	48	52	259
Cumbria	49	51	490
North Tyneside	53	47	281
Blackburn	48	52	854

[a] N: number of students in each category.

Table 3.12 provides a breakdown of the employment by sex, using the categories of current worker, former worker and never worked.

TABLE 3.12 Work status by sex: percentages.

	Current worker		Former worker		Never worked	
	Male	Female	Male	Female	Male	Female
Urban Scottish	38	32	30	27	32	40
Dumfries and Galloway	30	39	38	34	32	28
Cumbria	48	53	28	17	24	30
North Tyneside	33	60	44	20	23	20
Blackburn	27	36	22	15	50	49

In four out of five regions studied, somewhat more females are currently working than males. However, in the category of those who have work experience in the past, males outnumber females. (Other studies, which in the main, do not distinguish between current and former workers, generally find marginally more males have experience of work.) This might reflect the fact that employment participation for the two sexes differs depending on age. For example, males may typically start work at an earlier age but drop out of employment while females tend not to enter the part-time world of work until they are 14 or 15 years of age.

If this is the case then why the age differences in timing? One suggestion may be that there is an interaction between domestic duties and paid employment. Parents may be more likely to encourage males to seek experience outside of the home, or at least not inhibit this experience. In contrast, females are more likely to be 'protected' from the outside world for a longer period and may be required to carry out domestic roles instead.

That these hypotheses are not the sole explanation becomes evident when we realize that regional variations in the male–female pattern of employment exist. The urban Scottish sample has more males than females currently employed. This may be an indication that the types of jobs available in any area will influence the level of participation of males and females. This urban setting may provide the possibility for a large percentage of delivery types of work and these, in turn, may be male dominated.

Research has shown that the adult labour market divides along gender lines, this is also the case in the part-time employment of children.

Table 3.13 shows the jobs undertaken by those currently working. It is apparent that jobs such as delivery work are more likely to employ males, while others are female dominated, e.g. hawking, shop work, babysitting.

TABLE 3.13 Job types by sex: percentages

	URBSCO[a] M/F	DUMGAL[b] M/F	CUMBRIA[c] M/F	NTYNE[d] M/F	BLACKB[e] M/F
Delivery	86/14	86/14	85/15	85/15	81/19
Hawking	75/25	0/100	67/33	0/100	25/75
Shop work	32/68	21/79	27/73	13/87	32/68
Babysitting	0/100	6/94	2/98	6/94	7/93
Waiting	0/100	0/100	11/89	0/100	0/100
Farm work	–/–	100/0	100/0	100/0	–/–
Hotel and Catering	–/–	43/57	47/53	70/30	29/71
Other	36/64	73/27	68/32	58/42	42/58

[a] URBSCO: Urban Scottish.
[b] DUMGAL: Dumfries and Galloway.
[c] CUMBRIA: Cumbria.
[d] NTYNE: North Tyneside.
[e] BLACKB: Blackburn.

The data from all of the studies indicated that sex differences were found in other aspects of the experience of males and females involved in part-time work and we will turn to those shortly.

In considering the extent to which the current conclusions are supported by other research, we once again face methodological problems. Studies have paid differing degrees of attention to gender differences. Boyd (1994: 154) notes that 'in most discussions of labouring children, no distinction is made between the work of boys and girls'. While these comments were made within the context of a global perspective on child employment it is still a pertinent comment in the context of Britain. Where researchers have attended to gender differences the data still may not be directly comparable to our findings. Pond and Searle (1991) do not include babysitting as a job type and that is only one of many possible examples of divergence.

While bearing this limitation in mind we have re-analysed the data from other studies using some of our job category system. While this is not ideal, it does give us some indication of the extent to which the gender division of employment is mirrored in other research. Table 3.14 shows that in two key job areas, delivery and babysitting, there is general support for the idea of gender differentiation: boys tend to predominate in the former, girls in the later.

TABLE 3.14 Job type and sex: other studies.

	Delivery M/F	Shop work M/F	Babysitting M/F	Hotel and Catering M/F
Mizen	91/9	43/57	9/91	50/50
Pond and Searle	70/30	54/46	–/–	70/30
MacLennan et al.	79/21	59/41	–/–	62/38
Finn	63/37	46/54	0/100	40/60
Balding a	81/19	45/55	15/85	31/69
Balding b	35/65	35/65	17/83	23/77
Lavalette	86/14	36/64	17/83	–/–
Jolliffe et al.	68/32	50/50	–/–	66/34

In other categories the picture is less clear, for example waiting, and hotel and catering work. This could be attributed to different decisions being taken by researchers as to how to categorize jobs. For example, most studies do not make waiting a separate category. Lavalette supports our contention of this type of job being dominated by females but since this is the only study that employs this category, we need to be cautious about generalizing.

These results give only a rough guide to gender differences in child employment. Even when boys and girls are classified as doing the same type of job, more detailed analysis of the tasks set might show up differences.

At present our data supports the contention that job type is related to gender. Other research provided limited support for this and indicates the extent to which additional research is needed that pays attention to the variation in task demands within job categories.

No clear pattern appears if we attempt to differentiate the working hours of males and females. In three areas, boys tend to work longer hours; in the other two areas girls tend to work longer (see Table 3.15).

The problems of comparability between studies becomes evident once again when we look at the gender differences in the number of hours worked and pay

TABLE 3.15 Hours worked per week by sex.

	Male	Female
Urban Scottish	7.5	7.0
Dumfries and Galloway	9.5	8.1
Cumbria	9.2	7.1
North Tyneside	7.0	7.6
Blackburn	7.5	8.6

differentials between males and females. Few studies provide a breakdown of this data according to gender.

Davies's (1972) study did provide this data for category A and category B types of work. In category A employment, male average number of hours worked was longer than that for females. In category B employment, this pattern was reversed. It is important that one remembers that category B included domestic chores and child care, tasks in which females are more likely to be involved.

Two other studies provide a breakdown of hours worked and gender, Balding (1993) and MacLennan et al. (1985). In the former no differences were noted in the number of hours worked by the 14–15-year-old males and females in the study. In the latter study males worked longer hours than females. The picture is not at all clear.

However, gender differences were found when one considered the hourly pay rates. In each of the studies females predominated in the lowest pay category, whilst males were more likely to be in the higher hourly pay category compared to females. Comparable data is not available for Blackburn, but average hourly rates for males in Blackburn are greater than for females.

TABLE 3.16 Hourly earnings by sex: percentages.

	URBSCO[a] M/F	DUMGAL[b] M/F	CUMBRIA[c] M/F	NTYNE[d] M/F
Up to £1.00	42/58	33/67	32/68	10/90
£1.01–£2.00	36/64	33/67	26/74	50/50
£2.01–£3.00	60/40	25/75	69/31	57/43
£3.01 and over	100/0	–/–	100/0	33/67

[a] URBSCO: Urban Scottish.
[b] DUMGAL: Dumfries and Galloway.
[c] CUMBRIA: Cumbria.
[d] NTYNE: North Tyneside.

Are these differences due to the fact that girls tend to be in different jobs from boys? This is unlikely to be a major cause, since within almost all job categories male average rates of pay are higher than for females.

The lack of consistency in these studies and the failure of many studies to provide a suitable breakdown of their data means that we cannot find convincing support for our claim that males work more hours than females. A similar conclusion emerges when we turn attention on to the differential pay rates for males and females.

A number of studies do provide a breakdown of the hourly rates of pay for males and females and it must be noted that the trend that emerges is one that suggests males are paid more than females. This is the pattern in Davies (1972), Finn (1984) MacLennan et al. (1985) and Mizen (1992). While Balding (1993) does not provide a breakdown of hourly rates of pay for males and females he does supply us with enough information to carry this out. The youngest and oldest age groups males are paid more than females, while in the middle two age groups this differential is not apparent. Overall it must be concluded that more research is needed to assess the significance of this pattern.

LEGALITY OF EMPLOYMENT

As we have seen, according to the then British government, one of the reasons why Britain was justified in seeking an opt-out, for a limited period, from the European Union directive on child employment was because in Britain the current legislation is already satisfactory. The data collected in our studies hardly supports such a view.

The employment of children is regulated by the 1933 Children and Young Persons Act (and an equivalent 1937 Act for Scotland), some minor amendments to these Acts, and local authority bylaws made under the provision of the Acts. There are therefore two levels to this regulatory framework, central and local government.

The legislation sets the following framework for child employment. Children must

> be a minimum of 13 years of age;
> only work a maximum of 2 hours on a school day and Sundays;
> not work before 7.00 a.m. or after 7.00 p.m.;
> and not lift, carry or move objects likely to cause injury.

The Act also requires local authorities to consider how they are to regulate the system and provides for a permit system for this purpose. All of the authorities in the studies considered here had opted for a permit system. Thus, any child found working in any of our studies should have a valid permit.

In every district, the great majority of children were employed without the necessary permit. Note that, since our question asked the child if he or she had ever had a work permit, it may be that some of those who answered 'Yes' may have worked without one at some time. This serves only to stress even further the extent to which the law is not being enforced. When collecting the data for the various studies, we became aware of a widespread lack of awareness about this particular aspect of the law. This applies not only to children who work but also to adults who should be involved in the process, including teachers and local authority officials.

Table 3.17 does show a relatively higher level of permits held in the Dumfries and Galloway area than elsewhere. This was in part due to the fact that in one of the three schools in that area about half of the working pupils had permits. However, the other schools in Dumfries and Galloway also had higher than average permit

TABLE 3.17 Percentage of children who ever had a work permit.[a]

Urban Scottish	1
Dumfries and Galloway	29
Cumbria	6
North Tyneside	7
Blackburn	4

[a] Current and former workers.

rates. Since these schools were in a rural setting, it is possible to speculate that conformity to the permit system may be easier to establish and maintain in this type of community. However, this argument is clearly an oversimplification, since when one considers the level of permits recorded in the rural sector within the Cumbria study, it can be seen that permit holding was no more common than in any of the urban settings.

Further investigation of the schools in Dumfries and Galloway showed that they all placed a deliberate emphasis on providing information about the permit system to their pupils. The school with the highest permit rate was the most rigorous in pursuing this policy. The high permit rate thus probably reflects this proactive stance.

We need to be cautious in assuming that telling pupils about the regulations and permits necessarily transfers into action. This is evident from the fact that even in the school where the policy seemed most effective, the take-up rate was still less than perfect. After all around a half of the working pupils in that school had never had a work permit. The school deserves praise for its policy but the fact that it was only partially successful suggests that other factors must work against young workers obtaining a permit. We would argue that the problem lies with the nature of the permit system itself, and we will return to a discussion of this issue later.

The illegal nature of the employment experience is not limited to the lack of permits. As we have already reported, in every study we have found that children are employed outside the 7.00 a.m. and 7.00 p.m. watershed. In contrast to this situation, in which the start and finish times of a large percentage of working children fall outside that prescribed by legislation, there is less frequent breach of the law with respect to total hours worked. In each study only a small percentage of working children exceeded the legal maximum number of hours.

While it is possible to take some heart from this one needs to be cautious. A small number of children appear to work many longer hours than the law allows. In addition it should be noted that recent research in both America and Britain, which we shall discuss later, has indicated that even those children working within the legal framework may be working enough hours to increase the potential negative impact of employment on educational achievement.

A further area worth considering within a review of the legal status of child employment is age. The data we have been presenting focuses on pupils of 14 and 15 years of age. As such our respondents were above the legal minimum age. We have asked participants to provide us with information on their age when they first entered paid employment outside of the family. From their replies, it is evident that a number of children start work below 13 years, the legal minimum. Typically between a fifth and a third of all pupils with experience of paid employment say they started work before they were legally eligible to do so. The main problem with this data is that it is retrospective and one may suspect the accuracy of their recall. However it is possible to seek some indication of its reliability from other sources.

In Blackburn, children in the first year of secondary school were included in the sample. These school pupils will normally be about 12 years of age. While fewer pupils in the first year were working than in later years, 20 per cent were currently working and a further 8 per cent were former workers. Balding's (1993) data also indicated that children are employed in 'regular paid work' in the first year of secondary schooling.

The final issue to mention with respect to legality is the types of jobs done by children. We have already discussed the problems involved in researching this area. These can increase if we are attempting to decide whether any given job falls inside or outside the law. An example may clarify this. In the area of work generally described as hotel and catering work, delivering food to a table would fall within the law, while working in the kitchen would not. Many researchers have employed categories which do not permit such a distinction to be made. Our own questionnaire research techniques are probably not sensitive enough to allow us to draw firm conclusions on whether some jobs children report are legal or not. Other forms of data-collecting such as observational studies would be needed.

A further difficulty arises from the existence of local authority bylaws, which vary in what jobs they prohibit. Nevertheless, it can still be said that there is evidence that children find themselves working in prohibited areas. A number of the jobs which we placed in the 'other' category, when outlining the variations in children jobs previously, are clearly illegal. Examples of children working in a sawmill, as a garage mechanic and working on a fishing boat were found. It is also evident from the descriptions given by children of their work that many are working in environments which are prohibited, for example, working in the preparation of food.

The extent of work without permits or breaking some restriction which we have found is confirmed by other studies. MacLennan et al. state that 'the majority of children appear to be working illegally on one count or another' (1985: 27). They estimate that in their study four out of five children were working illegally. Jolliffe et al. (1995) adopt a similar approach and conclude that 88 per cent of the children working in their sample were employed illegally since they broke one or other of the regulations. Similarly, Pond and Searle (1991) express concern about the illegal nature of much child employment. In their study they estimate 74 per cent were working illegally, 33 per cent being involved in jobs that were prohibited. Infringements of the regulations relating to age of employment and the start and finishing times were also noted by Pond and Searle.

The overwhelming weight of this evidence leads us to the conclusion that the majority of children work illegally. The legislative framework is there to protect children but it is not implemented. One of the reasons for this is related to the 'invisible' nature of child employment. Over time in Britain, people seem to have convinced themselves that only a few children work and those who do so are engaged in entirely unproblematic jobs. The danger is that if children are not recognized as part of the workforce, a potential for exploitation exists.

In addition, this group of workers may suffer in other ways. If a child is employed without a permit then the issue of insurance cover enters a grey area. Are they covered in the event of accidental injury? The fact that children may find themselves in need of insurance cover becomes evident when we consider the extent of accidental injury arising from employment.

HEALTH AND SAFETY

In looking at the nature of children's work experience it is worth considering the potential risks that they face in terms of accidental injury at work. Table 3.18 indicates the number of children who had received some form of accidental injury while at work.

The data in Table 3.18 would appear to indicate that accidents are not uncommon in children's work experience. Other researchers in this area appear to share our concerns on this issue. From Table 3.19 we can see that a number of them have collected data on accidental injury at work as part of their research.

These studies might appear at first sight to show a strikingly consistent level of reported accidents. However, we need to bear in mind that these studies have

TABLE 3.18 Percentages reporting accidents at work.

Urban Scottish	18
Dumfries and Galloway	21
Cumbria	21
North Tyneside	23
Blackburn	19

TABLE 3.19 Percentages reporting accidents at work: other findings.

MacLennan et al.	31
Pond and Searle	35
Jolliffe et al.	36

employed different definitions of employment in their research and hence any consistency may be illusory. One may start to appreciate this fact when we compare these other studies with our own data. Whereas in our research, reported accidents range between 18 and 23 per cent of respondents, these other studies all found over 30 per cent of child workers reporting accidents. Variation in the level of recorded accidents is apparent. It is possible that contrasting methodology and definitions are influencing this.

The form of job types included in the research may be one of the variables which helps produce this variation. Pond and Searle (1991) exclude babysitting as a form of employment. If babysitting (and we must stress the 'if') is a form of employment where accidental injury is rare, studies which include those who work as babysitters will have lower overall accident rates than those which do not include babysitting.

A rather different impression is gained if we consider Health and Safety Executive records of accidents involving children under 16 years of age. Over the five-year period between 1990–91 and 1994–95, a total of only three fatal accidents were reported. Accidents requiring an absence from work of three days or more range between 30 and 58 per year (Health and Safety Commission, 1996). If our estimates of the number of children working at any given time as being well over a million are even approximately correct, the Health Safety Executive (HSE) figures would suggest a very low accident rate indeed. There is reason to believe that official accident figures may be underestimates, however. The HSE acknowledges that accidents generally tend to be underreported. In addition, since most children under 16 years of age are employed illegally, there would be a natural unwillingness to report accidents involving them.

There is also the issue of what counts as an accident. The HSE focus on more serious forms of accidents, notably fatalities or those involving absence for more than three days. Many accidents to children may fall outside of those categories. However, it is possible to argue that accidents which are treated as minor in adults may have greater impact in childhood or adolescence.

Is it the case that accidents are more likely to occur in certain jobs? Is it the case that most accidents occur in job categories that may be prohibited? In a recent study we have started to address these issues.

The data was collected to consider the possible relationship between job type and accidents. A self-report questionnaire was used asking pupils to provide information on their current and past employment. The pupils were also asked to provide specific information about any work-related accidents, to explain the circumstances and the job they were doing at the time of the accident.

The data was collected from three schools in Scotland (total sample size = 475, males = 53 per cent of sample, females = 47 per cent of sample). The schools involved were matched in terms of size of school, catchment area and socio-economic indicators such as free school meals and clothing grants. Mean age of the sample was 13.8 years. Of those who had ever worked, 19 per cent reported having had an accident at work, a figure comparable with the studies we had conducted previously.

TABLE 3.20 Accidents by type of job: percentages.

	School A	B	C	All
Delivery	56	57	72	62
Hawking	8	–	–	2
Shop work	–	5	6	4
Babysitting	–	14	6	7
Waiting	–	–	6	2
Farm work	–	–	–	–
Hotel and Catering	19	5	–	7
Other	19	19	11	16

It is apparent that the majority of accidents occur in delivery work, a form of employment which is often perceived as acceptable 'children's work'. The next highest number of accidents were reported in the 'other' category. These jobs included hairdressing, cleaning, kennel work, carer and working on a shooting range.

The types of accidents reported included broken legs, broken arms and fractured fingers. All of these 'breakages' should be recorded in the official HSE figures. To the best of our knowledge they were not reported. In addition, a range of other accidents were reported. These included burns, sprained ankles, numerous falls down stairs (and one from scaffolding), falling from bicycles, cuts from glass or sharp tools, dog bites, hit by car.

None of the latter would have been included in the HSE categories and would therefore not be officially recorded. However, what these figures do is display the potential for accidental injury among children at work and that it is in the supposedly 'acceptable' children's jobs that most accidents are recorded.

Farm work was not represented in this sample. This reflects the urban nature of the sample used. However, there is some evidence linking children and accidental injury on farms (Cameron et al., 1992). This shows the need for future research to encompass both rural and urban settings.

On the basis of this study it is clear that official figures may only be reflecting a small percentage of work-related accidents involving children. However, this study was carried out on a relatively small scale and its reliability needs to be checked. In particular the reliance upon retrospective recall of accidents by those involved may be problematic. To consider the accuracy of these findings it would be useful to adopt a range of methods for collecting data. For example hospital Accident and Emergency units and general practitioners could record work-related accidents for this age group. This, in turn, may lead to the development of a more useful system of recording and categorizing children's work-related accidents than the one we have at present.

In addition there is a need for epidemiological studies on the impact of work on children. To date there are no studies which consider the impact of work on the development of the child, for example, the long-term consequences of lifting weights, the effect of repetitive actions, the effect of coming into contact with chemicals when doses are regulated upon adult-based data? We also need to contextualize these accidents by comparing them to the 'everyday' accidents experienced by this population in general.

CONCLUSION

The aim of this chapter was to investigate the nature of child employment, to go beyond the numbers working and to consider what they actually do. It is apparent that children are employed in a wide range of jobs, many of which are more likely to be associated with the adult labour market than our notions of 'children's jobs'. In addition it can be argued that the child's gender may play a role in the types of jobs that are available to them, and that while there may be some evidence of differential pay rates for males and females, the overall rates of pay are generally low.

Perhaps the most disturbing aspect of this review has been the realization that the legislative system put in place to control child employment is not working. This becomes an important issue if we consider it alongside the evidence about the risk of accident associated with the employment experience.

We need to bear in mind that each of the studies referred to in this chapter, our own and those of other investigators, has been of the 'snapshot' variety. There is a dynamic element to child employment, however. Children move in and out of jobs; they change jobs. Snapshot studies can tell us little about this. In the chapter that follows, we shall follow some children over a longer period of time.

Chapter 4

A Closer Look at Cumbria

As was explained at the end of the previous chapter, there is a limit to what one may learn about child labour by questioning each child only once. Accordingly, it seemed to us worth while to take the opportunity to study the pupils in particular schools over a longer period of time. The chance arose in Cumbria.

Although Cumbria is best known in Britain, and probably around the world, because of the Lake District, made famous by association with the romantic poets, it is a county quite mixed in character. The population is around half a million, and there are two substantially sized towns, Carlisle (population around 72,000) and Barrow-in-Furness (population around 60,000). There are a further three towns with populations over 20,000: Kendall, Whitehaven and Workington.

The county is divided into six districts. Using the criterion of the percentage of the population living in towns of over 20,000 inhabitants, two districts, Barrow (100 per cent) and Carlisle (70 per cent) can be regarded as essentially urban, while the others, Copeland (36 per cent), Allerdale (29 per cent), Eden (29 per cent), and South Lakeland (25 per cent) can be regarded as essentially rural.

The two largest categories of employment in the county are services (over 50 per cent) and manufacturing (around 30 per cent). The main industrial centre has been Barrow, where manufacturing accounts for more than 50 per cent of jobs. However, in the period of this research, it faced a crisis, as jobs in shipbuilding were falling dramatically. In 1992 the government launched a Cumbrian Marketing initiative in an attempt to deal with the problems caused by job losses, not only in shipbuilding but in the nuclear power industry based at Sellafield in the Copeland district.

Unemployment in the county stood at 4.8 per cent in 1990, somewhat better than the average for England and Wales (6.4 per cent). In Barrow unemployment was 5.6 per cent, whereas in South Lakeland, where 64 per cent of jobs are in services, unemployment was only 2.1 per cent.

In 1992, and again in 1994, with the support of Cumbria County Council, we investigated the nature and extent of child employment in that county. The four schools selected for study each represented a different district, the two urban areas and two of the rural (Copeland and South Lakeland).

The percentages of students in each school who were in receipt of free school meals and clothing grants gives some indication of the relative levels of deprivation (see Table 4.1). They range from the Barrow school, where poverty indicators are relatively high, to the South Lakeland school, where poverty indicators are relatively low.

TABLE 4.1 Students receiving free school meals and clothing grants 1993/94: percentages.

School	Free school meals	Clothing grants
A Carlisle	18	15
B South Lakeland	6	6
C Barrow-in-Furness	38	48
D Copeland	14	17

This research was not originally planned as an integrated whole. Initially, the Educational Committee invited us to undertake a modified version of the 'snapshot' studies of the sort we have done elsewhere. Year 10 school students were surveyed in June 1992. The findings of that study were reported alongside those of other areas in the previous chapter. This initial study was supplemented by a further survey conducted of the same cohort in September 1992, by which time they were in Year 11. This showed that significant numbers of children, as in other areas, before the end of their compulsory school education, were employed in part-time jobs. The type of work done by these children covered a wide range of occupations and extended 'children's jobs' such as newspaper delivery. The great majority of children were employed illegally. There was some evidence that employment was associated with poorer educational performance and attendance.

These results were sufficiently interesting to the Education Committee for them to ask us to expand the study. By surveying a further cohort of school students, the representativeness of the first study was to be checked. In other words, were the earlier findings showing the normal levels of child employment in the region? In addition, fuller evidence on the relationship between education and part-time work was to be collected.

By extending the research we are able to compare similar groups at different points in time (i.e. Year 10 students in 1992 and 1994) and to follow the same group over time (as they move from Year 10 to Year 12).

The first element of the study involved Year 10 students completing questionnaires during June 1992 and June 1994. The format was identical in each year in order that legitimate comparisons could be made. The questionnaire asked for information on current and past employment, e.g. number of hours worked, type of job, rate of pay, work-related injuries and work permits. Staff were encouraged to follow up students who were absent on the day the questionnaires were completed to ensure a high completion rate. Table 4.2 shows the number of Year 10 students who participated in both the current and previous study. Although

TABLE 4.2 School students in Year 10 surveys.

School	Year 10 (1992)			Year 10 (1994)		
	N[a]	S[b](%)	M/F[c](%)	N[a]	S[b](%)	M/F[c](%)
A Carlisle	154	(81)	47:53	152	(80)	52:48
B South Lakeland	108	(94)	56:44	113	(75)	50:50
C Barrow-in-Furness	50	(72)	36:64	64	(74)	45:55
D Copeland	178	(83)	51:49	184	(78)	44:56
TOTAL	490	(83)	49:51	513	(77)	48:52

[a] N: number of students responding.
[b] S: respondents as percentage of students on roll.
[c] M/F: percentage of male and female respondents.

slightly more students completed the questionnaire in 1994, the return rate was slightly poorer.

The second investigation permitted us to undertake a longitudinal analysis of the work patterns of students over three school years, i.e. Year 10, Year 11 and Year 12. Employment data for students who were in Year 10 in June 1992 and in Year 11 in September 1992 was supplemented by data collected from the same cohorts who, in June 1994, were in Year 12.

As many Year 12 students were preparing for examinations, questionnaires were administered in March and April 1994. One of the participating schools did not have facilities for Year 12 students. However, with the aid of staff at the nearby Sixth Form College, we were able to identify students who were eligible to take part in the study through having been at the relevant school. The questionnaire addressed a number of issues related to current employment status such as number of hours worked per week and pay rates. Given that Year 12 students are less rigidly timetabled in comparison to other year groups, attendance data was not collected. Similarly, given the range of courses open to students, no performance data was collected either. However, GCSE results and attendance figures had been collected the previous year for the Year 11 sample in order to examine the potential impact of employment on school performance.

Table 4.3 represents the number of Year 11 and Year 12 students who completed questionnaires. Completion rates are again given in parentheses.

Obviously, the number of students in Year 12 has decreased substantially when compared with Year 11. Some students will have left school to find full-time employment; others may have moved outside the area or entered further education. Despite the low number of students in Year 12, the completion rates indicate that, with the exception of school B, the vast majority of eligible students completed questionnaires.

Although we surveyed the same cohort of students at three different points in their school careers, for a variety of reasons only a minority of the total sample completed all three questionnaires. However, although only a small proportion of

TABLE 4:3   Students in Year 11 and Year 12 surveys.

School	Year 11 (1992)			Year 12 (1994)		
	N^a	S^b(%)	M/F^c(%)	N^a	S^b(%)	M/F^c(%)
A Carlisle	169	(88)	49:51	34	(72)	44:56
B South Lakeland	108	(93)	53:47	62	(68)	52:48
C Barrow-in-Furness	51	(74)	37:63	9	(82)	22:78
D Copeland	166	(78)	45:55	61	(98)	46:54
TOTAL	494	(84)	47:53	166	(79)	46:54

[a] N: number of students responding.
[b] S: respondents as percentage of students on roll.
[c] M/F: percentage of male and female respondents.

TABLE 4.4   Composition of samples.

School	Year 10 N^a	Year 11 N^a	Year 12 N^a	Total	Answered all three Questionnaires N^a
A Carlisle	154	169	34		28
B South Lakeland	108	108	62		44
C Barrow-in-Furness	50	51	9		7
D Copeland	178	166	61		49
TOTAL	490	494	166	1150	128

[a] N: number of students responding.

those initially sampled, these pupils made up a fairly high proportion of those still at school in Year 12. Table 4.4 summarizes the samples.

INDIVIDUAL WORK HISTORIES

Before considering the statistics, let us look at some individual pupils and examine their work histories. Twelve people have been chosen to stress the variety of experience pupils may have.

George

We start with George because, although we are interested in pupils' part-time jobs, it is as well to keep in mind that some of them never work while at school.

George, who attends a South Lakeland school, is not interested in carrying on his education when he leaves. He wants to get a job when he leaves but does not have a clear idea of what kind of one. Each time he answered a questionnaire for us, George had no present or past job to report. He had never applied for a job and did not wish to work until he leaves school. For George, the divide between the schooling and working stages of one's life seems sharp.

Peter

Initially Peter, who attends a school in Copeland, appeared to be a 'non-worker' like George. He had no work experience to report when questioned in Years 10 and 11. He did say, however, that although he had had no summer job between Years 10 and 11, he would have liked to have had one. The following summer, he was successful in finding employment, as a catering assistant working 24 hours per week for £75.00. He left that job at the end of his holiday, but in Year 12 he had a rather different kind of work, playing two nights a week in a rock band. This earned him around £50.00 per week.

Peter's aim is to carry on his education after school and to work in a technical capacity in the film industry.

Jason

Jason, who attends a school in Carlisle and hopes to be a graphic designer, has a work history which contrasts sharply with George's. In Year 10, he reported currently having a job and having had three previous jobs. By Year 12, his total number of different jobs had risen to eight. He never had a work permit. Jason started work at the age of 12 on a paper round earning £9.00 per week. He subsequently had another paper round at £14.00 per week and a labouring job, in which he worked three hours for £5.00. His current job in Year 10 was another paper round (six days a week for £8.00) and he kept that job over the subsequent summer. He then moved to a Sunday paper round, in which he worked only four hours and earned £18.00. He then tried working in supermarkets. In one case he earned £35.00 per week for eight and a half hours' work as a produce assistant. He was made redundant. In the other, he stacked shelves for 17 hours per week for £45.00. He left because he 'hated the job and the place'. His current job when questioned in Year 12 was collecting glasses in a bar, six hours on Saturdays, earning £13.10.

Jason's varied work experience suggests that money was not his primary concern in seeking employment. The last of his four paper rounds was admittedly the best paid, but his previous paper round had had the lowest pay. He voluntarily gave up his best paid job of all.

Jennifer

Jennifer, who attends a school in Barrow-in-Furness and hopes to find work eventually in the media, offers a further contrast. She has worked steadily since the age of 13, but continuously in the same job. Jennifer went into a local bookshop and asked if there were any vacancies. She was interviewed and taken on to work around seven or eight hours on a Saturday. The pay is £10.00 and appears to have remained unchanged throughout the whole time she has had the job. Jennifer has not had a work permit. She has never had any other job. She feels that having had this work is beneficial to her job prospects when she leaves school, since it shows she is responsible, willing and hard working.

Karen

Like Jennifer, Karen thinks that having had part-time work while at school is likely to be an aid in seeking full-time employment later. She expresses her belief in the advantages to be gained from working with some feeling:

> Shows willing to try ... not afraid to meet new people ... do something constructive ... I will have had experience of a working day, mixed with more mature/experienced people, learnt to work with other people ... Had experience of dealing with money ... Money has greater value when earned.

Karen, whose aim is to be a solicitor, attends a South Lakeland school. She started work at age 12 and continued in some sort of employment through to Year 12, but never with a work permit. Her first job was as a waitress, earning £6.00 for two hours' work. In Year 10 she was working as a cleaner at a holiday complex, earning £15 for 5 or 6 hours' work one day a week. By Year 12 she was a 'Housekeeping Assistant' with similar hours and pay. She has also worked as a babysitter for various employers on a casual basis.

Anne

Anne attends a Copeland school. She has no clear idea of what she would like to do when she leaves school, other than to find some kind of job. When first questioned about her experience of work, she reported one previous job. At the age of 14, for four months she had been a waitress, working 10 hours and earning £24.00. She had no work permit. She does not say why she left that job. However, she appears not to have obtained any further employment, either during the holidays or in term time, during the two years of our enquiry.

Elaine

Elaine would like 'an office job' when she leaves school in Barrow-in-Furness. She comes near to George in her relative lack of work experience. When questioned in Year 10 she was earning about £5.00 per week as a babysitter. However, that seems to have been a fairly short-term arrangement. She did not report any subsequent work. Indeed, in Year 12, she reported that she had never had a job. One reason for this may show the fallibility of memory. Alternatively, it may display a shift in attitude. At a younger age, babysitting may feel like working. However, as she got older, her notion of what she regarded as a 'real' job may have become rather narrower. In Year 12, although without a job herself, she expressed a belief that having a part-time job helps one's future prospects.

Paul

Paul is a rare example of a worker who reports having a work permit. He is at school in Barrow-in-Furness and aspires to being a doctor. Throughout the period of our investigation he had the same job, delivering newspapers for two hours, one day a week, for about £3.60. Paul worked directly for the newspaper, which had taken responsibility for ensuring he had a work permit. Later, he had one other job, collecting glasses in a bar, earning £22.50 for 5 to 10 hours' work.

William

William's first job was on a milk delivery round. He earned £20.00 per week working a total of 21 hours. This job was illegal in three ways. He did not have a work permit; he was only 12 years old when he started; and he began work at 5.00 a.m. By the time we first questioned him in Year 10, he had given up that work but had a much less onerous job delivering newspapers, working about seven hours per week for £6.00. He later gave that up. During the summer holidays he worked as a glass collector in his grandparent's bar, earning £6.00 for four hours' work. This would not count as 'work outside the family' in our survey. However, he did not continue that job during term time as he said it would interfere with his school work. He hopes to work as a welder on leaving school.

John

Another person who worked as a glass collector in a bar was John. In Year 12, he was working two nights a week, sometimes until as late as 1.00 a.m. His weekly pay was just under £20.00. Presumably, unlike William, he saw this job as not threatening his school work. He had one previous job. Starting at the age of 12, he worked for three or four years delivering for a pharmacist. He worked one hour a day, six days a week. The pay rose over the years, eventually amounting to £15.00 per week. He had no work permit.

John is at school in Carlisle and hopes to continue his education after school and become an engineer.

Joan and Louise

We conclude these brief individual work histories by looking at Joan and Louise, both pupils at a Carlisle school and both hoping to become teachers. They had similar starts to their working lives. Joan started to babysit at the age of 13 (two and a half hours for £3.00). Louise at 14 (four hours for £5.00). When questioned in Year 10, Joan was working as a waitress (five hours' work for £10.00 plus tips); Louise on the other hand was still simply babysitting. Joan then went for some time without a job, having given up being a waitress because of 'lack of enjoyment'. In Year 12, she started work again in a job which combined the roles of waitress and shop assistant (10 hours per week for £25.00). Louise, on the other hand, had her first non-babysitting job in Year 11, working as a sales assistant. She carried on in this work into Year 12, earning £14.00 for an eight-hour day. Neither Joan nor Louise had a work permit at any time.

The main point to be made from these work histories is the impossibility of being able to specify a 'standard' pattern. Most work could be classified as 'service' in a broad sense (delivering, waiting, selling, cleaning, for example). Most workers do not have the permits they should have prior to the age of 16. There is a general trend for work to become more common as pupils become older, but there are exceptions. Elaine tried babysitting for a time, but subsequently was jobless. Anne gave up working after a few months as a waitress. Some workers, like Jason, move frequently between jobs. Others, like John and Paul, find a job and stick with it. Rates of pay vary quite a lot, but there is little evidence that people change jobs primarily in search of more money. Dislike of a job is a more frequently stated reason for leaving. Only George, who was one of the minority who do not work at all, can be said to fit a fixed pattern.

These case histories have been chosen to show the variety of experiences pupils may have of work. They are not meant to be representative. To consider general trends we need to examine the overall statistics. However, it is worth bearing in mind the complex variety of individual stories that lie behind the averages and percentages which we shall be discussing.

CHILD EMPLOYMENT IN CUMBRIA, FROM 1992 TO 1994

To what extent is child labour a relatively stable feature of the Cumbrian economy?

Overall, in the total sample of Year 10 school students there were marginally fewer students in employment in 1994. Within the individual schools it is interesting to note that school C, which has the most deprived catchment area and which had one of the highest employment levels in 1992, experienced a substantial decrease in the number of students in employment two years later.

Analysis of the data confirms that there was no significant difference in the number of students in employment in the sample as a whole over the two-year

TABLE 4.5 Work status of Year 10 students: percentages.

School	Current workers		Former workers		Never worked	
	1992	1994	1992	1994	1992	1994
A Carlisle	41	41	25	26	34	33
B South Lakeland	75	65	13	22	12	13
C Barrow-in-Furness	70	41	20	34	10	25
D Copeland	38	40	27	17	35	43
TOTAL[a]	50	46	22	23	27	31

[a] 'Total' refers to per cent of each category for the whole sample.

period. This would suggest that at any given time approximately one half of Year 10 school students in Cumbria will be in some form of paid employment. Figures for the individual schools ranged from 42 per cent to 66 per cent, reflecting the differing circumstances prevailing in the local economies.

In addition to current employment details, students were asked about previous jobs. The slight overall decrease in the number of current workers over the two-year period is matched by a marginal increase in the number of students who have never worked.

Table 4.6 Types of jobs currently undertaken by Year 10 students: percentages.

	1992	1994
Delivery	25	35
Hotel/catering	20	16
Babysitting	17	12
Shop work	17	9
Waiting	7	13
Farm work	<1	<1
Hawking	4	2
Other	10	13
TOTAL[a]	100	100

[a] 'Total' is to indicate that the percentages are of each column.

There has been a shift in the *nature* of the jobs over the two-year period. Delivery jobs, the most common form of child employment, increased by almost 10 per cent over the period of study. The number of students employed in waiting work almost doubled. The proportion of jobs classified as 'other' increased in part because of a rise in the number of students working as cleaners. Further examples of jobs in this category included: stable hand, window cleaner, lifeguard, office assistant and line assistant in a factory. In contrast, hotel and catering jobs, babysitting and shop work all decreased. There was no change in the number of students working in farm jobs, which was very small in both years.

There are a number of possible explanations for these changes. They may be random variations. They may be due to changes in attitudes or in the local economic conditions. The nature of the study means that we are not in a position to allow any one of these to be verified.

It is also possible that these changes could be explained best by considering variations within individual schools. Table 4.7 covers the jobs held by students in each participating school.

The clearest change in school A (Carlisle) was that delivery jobs increased by 16 per cent. There is a small rise in shop work (against the regional trend). Babysitting experienced the largest decrease.

Table 4.7 Types of jobs currently undertaken by Year 10 students: percentages in each school.

School	A		B		C		D	
	1992	1994	1992	1994	1992	1994	1992	1994
Delivery	35	51★	4	8	20★	42	41	43
Hotel/catering	10	8	55★	36	–	8	–	5
Babysitting	16★	5	1	1	51★	31	18	22
Shop work	10	13	26★	6	14	8	15	11
Waiting	14	11	4	22★	–	4	9	10
Farm work	–	–	1	–	–	–	–	1
Hawking	6	3	–	–	9	4	3	3
Other	10	10	9	26★	6	4	15★	5
TOTAL[a]	100	100	100	100	100	100	100	100

Changes of more than 10 per cent in an occupation for a school group are indicated by an asterisk(★) beside the greater.
[a] 'Total' is to indicate that the percentages are of each column.

The largest changes at school B (South Lakeland) were within the service sector. Hotel and catering work, which accounted for over half of the jobs in 1992 fell to just over a third of all jobs. Shop work also fell, but waiting increased.

In 1992 babysitting was the most common form of employment in school C (Barrow-in-Furness), with just over 50 per cent of students recording this as their main source of employment. However, the figure for babysitting dropped by almost a half two years later. Delivery jobs, which approximately doubled, became the most common source of employment. Hotel and catering, and waiting jobs, not recorded at all in the earlier study, accounted for just over 10 per cent of jobs in 1994. The proportion of female students who completed questionnaires in this school in 1994 was lower in comparison to 1992. This may account for some of the shifts, including that from babysitting to delivery work as the most commonly reported job.

School D (Copeland) is the one which shows the greatest stability in the distribution of jobs. There are no particularly striking differences in terms of work done by students in the two survey years. The two largest sources of employment, delivery and babysitting, both showed marginal increases.

Thus, individual schools vary not only in the pattern of jobs typically undertaken by students but also in the extent to which there are changes in that pattern over the years. Whilst it is interesting to speculate on possible causes, these details should not distract us from the broad, general findings, namely that most students work before the official school-leaving age and the level of employment remains fairly constant overall.

Hours Worked

Given that these surveys were carried out during term time it is possible to be precise about the number of hours school children are permitted to work. The bylaws for regulating the employment of children in Cumbria assert that during schooldays children may not be employed for more than two hours. At weekends, hours are limited to two on a Sunday, between 7.00 a.m. and 11.00 a.m. and either five or eight hours on a Saturday, dependent on whether the child has reached 15 years of age. The maximum number of hours permitted during term time is thus 17 for under-15s and 20 hours for students aged 15 or over.

TABLE 4.8 Hours worked per week by Year 10 students: percentages.

	1992	1994
5 hours or less	36	38
6–10 hours	41	45
Over 10 hours	22	17
TOTAL[a]	100	100

[a] 'Total' is to indicate that the percentages are each column.

The percentage of students working in excess of 10 hours per week was 17 per cent in 1994 compared with the slightly higher figure of 22 per cent in 1992. The overall drop in the number of students working in excess of 10 hours per week was repeated throughout the individual schools. In the other two categories findings were mixed. Schools C and D had more students working five hours or less in the follow-up survey, while in schools A and B the number of students working between 6 and 10 hours rose. The maximum number of hours recorded was 30 hours per week in both 1992 and 1994. Less than 2 per cent of students were working more hours than permitted by the bylaws.

The bylaws, in addition to regulating the number of hours worked per week, control when children's part-time work starts and ends. Children are not allowed to work before 7.00 a.m. in the morning or after 7.00 p.m. at night. Table 4.9 suggests that this particular aspect of the bylaws is perhaps the most frequently ignored.

Over a third of the current sample who had ever worked did so before the 7.00 a.m. limit. This represents an increase from the previous study and is

TABLE 4.9 Start and finish times of Year 10 students: percentages.

School	Starting before 7.00 a.m.		Finishing after 7.00 p.m.	
	1992	1994	1992	1994
A Carlisle	46	55	39	43
B South Lakeland	9	4	67	67
C Barrow-in-Furness	22	47	50	58
D Copeland	33	49	45	60
TOTAL[a]	28	36	51	57

[a] 'Total' referes to per cent of each category for the whole sample.

particularly marked in school C. It is worth bearing in mind that the type of work children do will influence the starting and finishing time of employment. Thus the increase in school C is most likely related to the increase in the number of delivery jobs.

More than half of the students who had worked had done so beyond the evening restriction of 7.00 p.m. The 1994 figures show that more students than in 1992 were working at times of the day defined as illegal.

Earnings

Overall, in 1994 there was a slight decrease in the number of students earning under £2.00 per hour in the current sample. Students earning over £3.00 per hour more than doubled over the study period. This pattern was generally repeated throughout the schools with the exception of school D. Although the differences between the hourly earnings in both survey years was marginal, in this school slightly more students were earning £1.00 or less while slightly fewer earned over £3.00 per hour.

The most striking finding was in school C where no students earned over £3.00 in 1992 in contrast to 20 per cent of students in the current study. The lowest wage rate recorded was 43 pence per hour. Mean hourly and weekly earnings for both studies are given in Table 4.10.

TABLE 4.10 Average earnings.

School	£'s per hour 1992	£'s per hour 1994	£'s per week 1992	£'s per week 1994
A Carlisle	2.12	1.93	12.64	14.14
B South Lakeland	2.49	2.87	20.82	22.43
C Barrow-in-Furness	1.38	2.16	10.03	10.20
D Copeland	1.91	2.05	13.79	12.46
TOTAL	2.11	2.29	15.20	15.66

With the exception of school A, the average hourly rate has increased. This increase is particularly marked in school C and may be explained by the change in job profiles over the period. Average hourly rates rose by about 8 per cent, but because of the slight decline in average hours worked, the rise in average weekly wages was only 3 per cent. The trends in pay seem to suggest an overall stability, since the increases are close to what one might expect to come about through inflation.

Age

Children are not permitted by statute to work before the age of 13. In some local authorities, including Cumbria, an exception is made for children aged between

10 and 13 years of age who are employed with a parent in agricultural work, an area of activity which has little significance for the students in these surveys.

The findings from the 1992 study showed that over a third of students had reported having worked before reaching the minimum age of 13. In 1994 slightly fewer students had started working before the legal age limit (28 per cent). The majority in both instances reported having their first paid job at the age of 12.

Work Permits

Work permits are the key regulatory mechanism for controlling child employment. In theory, children are not permitted to work without one. The procedure for obtaining a work permit usually involves the participation of child, employer, parent, school and in some instances, general practitioner. In 1992, only 7 per cent of pupils who had worked had ever had a work permit. The figure for 1994 marginally improved to 10 per cent. Thus in this respect the majority of working children in Cumbria remain illegally employed. Schools A, C and D experienced an increase in the number of students who had had a permit for current or past jobs. The figure for school C (Barrow-in-Furness) in particular more than doubled. However, it nonetheless represents only a small minority of working students.

Accidents

As we have noted previously, children working illegally without permits may not be protected by standard employee insurance cover. Table 4.11 demonstrates the significance of such a protection mechanism, given the substantial number of students who have suffered a work-related injury.

TABLE 4.11 Students reporting having had an accident at work: percentages.

School	1992	1994
A Carlisle	17	26
B South Lakeland	31	16
C Barrow-in-Furness	11	21
D Copeland	19	29
TOTAL	21	23

While the overall number of accidents has increased marginally, the responses from individual schools over the study period vary substantially. The level of accidents has increased in all but school B, where interestingly accidents at work have halved. These changes may be related to the shifts in patterns of employment.

There is a tendency for children to understate the extent of their injury or accident by adding comments like, 'it didn't really hurt' or 'it wasn't much of a cut'. Adult employees are required by the Health and Safety at Work Act 1974 to record all accidents at work and the same law applies to children. Whether child workers are aware of their rights as employees is however a matter for further research and discussion.

The most common examples of the accidents reported in this study included burns and cuts in catering jobs. Delivery work was generally associated with falling off bicycles and dog bites, including one student who was bitten badly and required hospital treatment. A small number of students were 'beaten up' and robbed on delivery rounds.

Gender

Table 4.12 compares the gender composition of job categories for the total sample in both survey years.

TABLE 4.12 Breakdown of job type by gender.

	1992			1994		
	N^a	M	F^b	N^a	M	F^b
Delivery	60	51	9	81	64	17
Hotel/catering	49	23	26	37	13	14
Babysitting	41	1	40	28	3	25
Shop work	41	11	30	22	1	21
Waiting	18	2	16	31	3	28
Farm work	1	1	0	1	1	0
Hawking	9	6	3	5	1	4
Other	25	17	8	30	19	11
TOTAL	244	112	132	235	105	120

[a] N: number of students in each category.
[b] M/F: number of male and female students in each category.

Note that although in both 1992 and 1994, marginally more female students were working compared with males, this reflects almost exactly the slightly higher proportion of females among those surveyed. Females predominate in waiting, shop work, babysitting, and hotel and catering, whilst males were predominant in delivery work. The gender stereotyping of jobs is broadly of the same extent in both years. The number of boys in shop work fell from 11 to 1 (strengthening the gender bias in that sort of work), whereas the number of girls in delivery work rose from 9 to 17 (a slight weakening of the gender bias).

Findings in 1992 showed that on the whole male students earned a higher average hourly rate (£2.23) than their female counterparts (£2.03). However, in 1994 we found that hourly earnings for female students slightly exceeded that of males, the average being £2.32 and £2.24 respectively.

Detailed analysis of a number of variables found significant patterns emerging in both years studied. These include:

- Male students are more likely to have worked.
- Male students are more likely to have reported having had an accident at work.
- Male students are more likely to have stayed off school to go to work or missed a class as a result of working.
- Female students are more likely to work one or two days per week as opposed to male students who tend to work six to seven days per week.
- Related to the above, male students are more likely to start work prior to 7.00 a.m. This and the above point may be related to the predominance of male students in delivery jobs.
- Male students are more likely to enter employment at an earlier age.

The findings discussed above do suggest that gender influences the experience of children in the labour market.

Comparison of School Years 10 to 12

Table 4.13 clearly demonstrates that as students progress through the final years of schooling, the number who have never worked decreases. By the time of reaching Year 12 the number who have never worked is slight, only 13 per cent. In other words, the overwhelming majority of school students will have had at least one paid job before leaving secondary education.

TABLE 4.13 Work status of students in surveyed school years: percentages.

	Current worker	*Former worker*	*Never worked*
Year 10	50	22	27
Year 11	50	30	20
Year 12	60	26	13

A total of 128 students answered all three questionnaires. Of this group, 67 were working when we surveyed them in Year 10. Following through to Year 11, we found 84 per cent remained in employment. In Year 12, 70 per cent were still working. Once a student has started working, more often than not, that student remains in employment.

On the whole, differences between Year 10 and Year 11 were small. Clearer differences, however, start to emerge when the types of job reported by Year 12 students are considered. It was noted previously that delivery jobs were the most commonly reported category of employment for Year 10 students (1992, 25 per cent; 1994, 35 per cent). The proportion of students in Year 11 who recorded this as their current form of employment was slightly smaller (24 per cent). By Year 12, the figure for delivery jobs had dropped substantially to only 3 per cent.

Hawking, farm work and babysitting were not recorded at all in the Year 12 sample. Just under half of Year 12 students were employed in shop work (46 per cent). Jobs categorized as 'other' were the next most common category. These included: cleaner, care worker, labourer and cellar manager.

It is perhaps of no surprise that the findings above suggest that as the age of students increases the type of work more closely reflects adult jobs. The popular stereotype of the newspaper boy or girl is not applicable to older school students. Having noted the difference in the types of jobs held by school students over the three school years, it is worth examining any potential relationship between types of job and the number of hours worked. It might be expected that jobs more commonly associated with the adult labour market demand more in terms of working hours.

No information was collected for current work hours in Year 11; however, the hours worked during the preceding summer vacation were investigated. Statistical analysis of the relationship between the number of hours worked in Year 10 and hours worked in holiday jobs, i.e. in the period between Year 10 and Year 11, found a positive correlation. In short, those students who worked longer hours in Year 10 were also likely to work longer hours in their holiday jobs. No relationship was found in a comparison of Year 10 hours and Year 12 hours. One possible interpretation of this finding is that those working long hours in Year 10 were most likely to leave school and hence were not represented in the Year 12 sample. Analysis confirmed that students working over 10 hours per week in Year 10 were indeed most likely to have left school.

Whilst there were considerably more Year 12 students working between 6 and 10 hours per week in comparison with the Year 10 sample, the figures for the over 10 hours category are indistinguishable. The mean number of hours worked per week was 8.1 for Year 10 and 8.8 for Year 12, indicating that on the whole Year 12 students are not making a much greater time commitment to paid work despite the change towards more 'adult' types of employment over the three years studied.

In summary, while Year 12 students are more likely to be employed in jobs associated with the adult labour market it would appear that, in terms of the number of hours worked per week, the demands are little greater than those experienced by Year 10 students.

CONCLUSIONS

This study has offered the rare opportunity to consider the issue of child employment from a different perspective. All previous studies within Britain have adopted a 'snapshot' approach, considering the nature and extent of child employment at a specific moment in time.

The comparison of Year 10 students in the same schools in 1992 and 1994 allows certain questions to be answered.

1. Has the level of employment changed? No, there is evidence of a remarkable consistency in the number of children working.
2. Are there still variations within different parts of the region? Yes, the results suggest that the types of jobs and the numbers working reflect the demands of regional economies.
3. Are children still working in the same range of jobs? Yes. While there is some re-distribution of the numbers working in different sectors children are still to be found working in a wide range of jobs.
4. Has the level of illegal employment changed? No. Unfortunately the majority of children are still working illegally, either because they have no work permit, are working outside prescribed hours or are working in prohibited jobs.

The second part of the study focused on a single cohort of students as they moved through the school system from Year 10 towards their first major set of examinations at the end of Year 11, the decision to leave school or continue on to Year 12, where A-level preparation begins.

What is most striking about the employment levels in Years 10 and 11 is the consistency in the number of students working. A somewhat higher percentage of students working was found in Year 12, 60 per cent. Since students are beginning preparation for A-levels, one might have anticipated that fewer students in this year would work. A-level preparation takes place over two years and it might be that while working is common in Year 12 it may be less common when these students enter Year 13.

The results also indicate that there is a hierarchy of employment among school students. The earlier years of student employment are dominated by delivery-style jobs, while the later years are dominated by more adult jobs. Very few of the Year 12 students were involved in delivery work, while shop work is the most common form of employment. We also find that Year 12 students are working in a wide range of jobs, including care workers, labourers and cleaners.

It is important to bear in mind that by Year 12 these students are no longer covered by the child employment legislation and are free to compete in the adult labour market. That they do this is evident from the range of jobs that are covered. However, the time commitment made by Year 12 students is in line with that made in the earlier school years with the majority working for 10 hours or less per week.

We also took the opportunity to examine the relationship between the work patterns of pupils in Cumbria and their schooling. Our findings here, along with other studies conducted in Scotland, are considered in the following chapter.

Chapter 5

WORK AND EDUCATION

BACKGROUND

The relationship between work and education is at the heart of many of the disputes about child employment. The possibility that time spent at work may have a harmful effect on the child's schooling is one of the key anxieties of many who wish to strictly control child labour. On the other hand, there is the suggestion that, for some children at least, a more meaningful education may be obtained at the workplace than in the school. These arguments are not easily resolved because they are frequently based on unstated assumptions about the aims of education. As far as Britain is concerned, there is the added problem that little relevant evidence has been collected.

We have already referred to the study carried out by Davies (1972) for the Department of Health and Social Security. Davies attempted to explore the relationship between work and education, and concluded that the number of hours of paid employment were linked unfavourably to various educational variables. Unfortunately, the information provided in the published version of the report gives insufficient detail. Davies wrote that he had conducted an analysis of variance on the association between hours per week in employment and seven educational variables: Ability, Industry, Behaviour, Attendance, Non-truancy, Punctuality and Attitude to school-leaving age. For boys, he found significant negative relations for all seven variables. For girls, the relationship was significantly negative, too, except in the case of Ability and Non-truancy. With the exception of 'Attitude to school-leaving age', these variables seem to have been measured by the assessments of teachers 'who were well acquainted with the pupils'. We are not told how carefully the teachers' acquaintance with each pupil was established. There seems to have been no check made on the validity of the teachers' judgements by, for example, relating 'Ability' to actual examination performance.

Davies was cautious in the conclusion he drew. In particular, he stressed that he had not demonstrated 'cause and effect'. He did not spell out his reason for saying this, but it may be worth suggesting at this point what he had in mind. If children who work longer hours do less well at school and seem less committed to schooling than those who work less or not at all, it is possible that this is because spending a longer time at work interferes with homework, makes one more tired, distracts one from school, and so on. However, there are other ways of explaining the relationship. Lack of commitment to school may *precede* involvement in work. It may be that those who are least involved in their school work are the most likely to seek out and undertake the more substantial jobs. A final reason for caution is that the likelihood of working longer hours and the likelihood of poor commitment to school are both the result of general social disadvantages such as poverty.

Although a certain amount of research evidence has been emerging in the United States which throws light on these issues, when we began researching child labour in Britain, the Davies study was the only one available. It seemed to us that the collection of additional evidence on this question was necessary. We first undertook a pilot study in Scotland and then developed rather fuller investigations in Scotland and Cumbria. There is still room for much more exploration of this area, but we believe these studies do go some way to clarifying this tricky question.

PILOT STUDY: URBAN SCOTLAND

Our first attempt to re-examine the issues raised by Davies involved students in their fourth year of secondary education at two urban Scottish schools. Although the schools were geographically close to each other, they differed in the social character of their catchment area. One, which we shall call Aberford, had fewer students receiving free school meals and clothing allowances than the other, which we shall call Bartown.

Of fourth year students at Aberford, 96 per cent (194) completed questionnaires; 75 per cent (153) of the corresponding Bartown students did so. The poorer completion rate at Bartown is probably due to the fact that the questionnaire was administered rather closer to the onset of examination preparation.

TABLE 5.1 Extent of work experience: percentages.

Employment category	Aberford	Bartown
Current worker	36	34
Former worker	30	28
Never worked	35	39

There was no evidence here that relative poverty is a major factor in child employment, since a slightly higher proportion of students at the more affluent school had jobs. However, one must be cautious, since the higher proportion of Bartown students not completing the questionnaire (because they were not at school) may have included some who were absent for employment-related reasons.

Our main interest here, however, was not amount of work in itself, but rather its possible effect on education.

TABLE 5.2 Work and attendance: percentages.[a]

Employment category	Aberford		Bartown	
	Male	Female	Male	Female
Current worker	93	94	92	92
Former worker	93	91	88	90
Never worked	92	93	92	94

[a] A figure of 100 per cent would represent perfect attendance.

When we considered attendance records supplied by the school we could find no significant differences in the attendance levels of the three employment categories. However, we also considered answers to a question about playing truant, 'dogging' school, as it is called locally. We found that those who were in the category of former workers were more likely to report having truanted than either current workers or those who had never been workers. This could be explained in different ways. It may be that workers actually truant more than non-workers, but that former workers are less reticent about admitting it than current workers. Another possibility is that a record of truanting may have contributed to a decision by some former workers to give up working, either as a personal decision or under pressure from parents or teachers. This outcome does provide us with a useful reminder that it is dangerous to lump together all children who have ever had jobs and compare them en bloc with the rest. It also raises a more general question: why do children become former workers?

The schools provided us with teachers' predictions of students' performance in the forthcoming Standard Grade Examinations. We focused on the two key subjects of Mathematics and English, comparing the mean predicted grades for the various groups. (The lower the grade, the better the performance.)

TABLE 5.3 Work and English performance.

	Mean grade			
	Aberford		Bartown	
Employment category	Male	Female	Male	Female
Current worker	2.8	2.3	3.1	3.0
Former worker	2.8	2.4	4.0	3.2
Never worked	3.0	2.5	3.3	3.0

An analysis of variance shows Aberford students significantly better than Bartown and girls significantly better than boys, but no significant difference on the basis of experience of employment.

In Mathematics, Aberford also shows up significantly better than Bartown, but there is no significant sex difference. There is a difference between the employment categories in this case, current workers being significantly better than the others.

TABLE 5.4 Work and Mathematics performance.

	Mean grade			
	Aberford		Bartown	
Employment category	Male	Female	Male	Female
Current worker	2.7	2.2	3.4	3.4
Former worker	2.9	2.7	4.5	4.1
Never worked	3.2	3.0	3.7	3.7

Finally, when we looked at students' intention to continue their education after the end of schooling, we found at Aberford only that those who had never worked were more likely to state that they planned to further their education.

This last result is the sole (but partial) confirmation of the Davies thesis that employment is associated with poorer academic performance and weaker commitment to education. For official attendance figures and English performance we found no support for this view. For Mathematics performance, we actually found a contrary result, since those currently working are better than the non-workers. (Fuller details of the pilot study may be found in Hobbs et al., 1993a).

This was a small scale investigation. It would not have been appropriate to abandon the Davies position on this evidence alone. Nevertheless, it did suggest that the Davies study from the 1970s might not necessarily be a good guide to the current situation and that more needs to be found out about what seemed increasingly likely to be the complex relationship between schooling and employment.

SECOND STUDY: URBAN AND RURAL SCOTLAND

Our next study had some basic similarities with the pilot. Once again we worked in Scotland, we asked students to complete questionnaires and we obtained attendance figures from the schools. However, there were also some changes. There were more schools (six). Half of the schools were urban and half rural. We looked at actual Standard Grade results across the board (as opposed to predicted performance in only Mathematics and English). Finally, we decided to take into account the number of hours per week reported by those currently working. This last was a factor mentioned by Davies, but he does not make clear how he built it into his analysis. We divided current workers into three categories: low hours (working 5 hours or less), moderate hours (working over 5 and up to 10 hours), and high hours (those working over 10 hours per week). The fact that some significant differences did emerge between these sub-groups confirms the value of exploring this factor.

The measures of educational performance used were based on the Standard Grade Examination results achieved by individual students. Examining performance on individual subjects was felt to be of limited value given that the range of options available differed between schools. For ease of analysis we decided to standardize the measure of performance in the form of a score for each student. Scottish Standard Grades vary from Grade 1 (highest) to Grade 7 (lowest). These were converted as follows: Grade 1 scores 7, Grade 2 scored 6 and so on. A student's scores in the various subjects assessed were then combined. Thus the higher the grades achieved by a student and the larger the number of subjects in which success was achieved, the higher the global score. (Information on numbers in particular subjects will be found in Appendix 3.)

Commitment to education was assessed on the basis of answers to certain items in the questionnaire and also two objective measures. The former covered the following points:

1. Whether the pupil intended to find employment on leaving school or proceed to further/higher education.
2. Whether the pupil had ever truanted from school.

Students with experience of employment were also asked whether they had ever missed school to go to work, stayed off school because they had been working (for example, too tired to go to school), or missed a class because of work (for example, missed the first class in the morning or left school before the last class of the day).

The objective measures of commitment to education were:

1. Attendance: an objective measure of commitment was supplied by the schools in the form of students' attendance records in Year S4.
2. Progression: i.e. whether or not a student entered Year S5.

Not one of these variables could in itself be regarded as a pure measure of commitment to education. However, each could potentially tell us something of the rival strengths for the pupil of the pulls of work and school. Some previous research on truancy (e.g. Gray and Jesson, 1990) has concluded that official attendance records are not necessarily the best guides to pupils' actual behaviour, hence the use of subjective measures in addition to the official figures.

It was found that answers to these questions tended to be related in the expected ways. Of the 21 comparisons between the variables which are possible, 15 showed significant positive relationships. Each variable showed an association with at least three of the other variables. This would support the notion that each in some degree is affected by an underlying commitment to education. (See Table 5.5)

Attendance figures for current workers with low weekly hours were found to be significantly better than all other groups. There were no other significant differences found in attendance, although those who worked the longest hours had marginally poorer average attendance figures. (See Table 5.6)

TABLE 5.5 Commitment to education measures.

		Related to other variables	
		Highly**	Moderately*
1	Returned to S5	2,3,4,5	
2	Not truanted	1,3,4,6	7
3	Plans continued education	1,2,4	6
4	Attendance	1,2,3,6	5
5^	Not missed school to work	1,6,7	4
6^	Not off school after work	2,4,5,7	3
7^	Not missed class after work	5,6	2

Statistic: Chi Squared
* $p < .05$.
** $p < .01$.
^   Applies only to students with work experience.

TABLE 5.6 Work and attendance: percentages.

Employment category	Average attendance
Current worker: low hours	94.5
Current worker: moderate hours	91.8
Current worker: high hours	91.2
Former worker	92.1
Never worked	93.0

TABLE 5.7 Work and return to school in S5: percentages.

Employment category	Average return to S5
Current worker: low hours	85.6
Current worker: moderate hours	75.6
Current worker: high hours	66.0
Former worker	75.6
Never worked	79.8

 Pupils currently working five hours a week or less not only have the best attendance, they were more likely to return to S5, were less likely to have truanted, expressed more interest in continuing education, and had less work-related absences than those working longer hours. Current workers with low hours also showed up favourably in comparison with former workers and those who had never worked. In contrast, those who have never worked show up favourably in comparison with those working longer hours, being 'second best' to 'low hours' workers on all four relevant variables. The other variables do not apply to those who have never worked.

 Turning now to academic performance, we found the most successful group to be current workers with low weekly hours (see Table 5.8). They perform significantly better than all other groups. Those who have never worked are the next most successful group, performing significantly better than former workers and those currently working more than 10 hours per week. Thus there is a similar pattern to that found when we compared the commitment to education of the various work status groups.

TABLE 5.8   Work and Academic Performance.

Employment category	Mean score
Current worker: low hours	40.9
Current worker: moderate hours	35.6
Current worker: high hours	33.4
Former worker	35.6
Never worked	37.9

Research in the United States suggests that it is not whether or not a pupil works which has an effect on his or her schooling but rather the nature of that work. The most obvious characteristic of a child's job is the number of hours worked, and it is that aspect on which we have concentrated so far. However, it should not be assumed that hours worked is the only potentially important variable. The specific types of activity involved in a job could also be important, for example, the amount of physical effort or the amount of responsibility taken. Even if we consider the times of day when the pupil is working there is the possibility of some influence on education. Although contrary to law, some pupils start work before 7.00 a.m. and others stop work after 7.00 p.m. Anecdotal evidence suggests that one of the clearest signs that a teacher may have that a pupil's schooling is under threat from a job is tiredness in class. Early starting and late finishing might be major causes of such tiredness.

It is important to note a potentially crucial difference in the wording of the question about hours worked on the one hand and the questions on starting and finishing times on the other. Workers were asked for a general statement about how much they worked, to which they might reasonably be expected to answer by describing their most common experience:

How many hours do you work per week?

In contrast the other questions referred to the pupil's most extreme experience:

What is the earliest time you have started work in the morning?
What is the latest time you have finished work at night?

The pupils' answers may not necessarily indicate what their most common starting and finishing times might be. Yet regular early starts, for example, are more likely to have an impact on education than the occasional early start.

One possibility is that early starting and late finishing is most common amongst those who work longest hours. However, analysis found no significant differences between the work groups in either early starts or late finishes.

Starting and finishing times did not appear significantly related to educational performance.

TABLE 5.9 Start and finish times and academic performance.

	Mean performance
Earliest start:	
Up to 7.00 a.m.	34.8
After 7.00 a.m	36.5
Latest finish:	
Up to 7.00 p.m	36.9
After 7.00 p.m	36.2

No significant differences were found in any of these variables when latest finishing times were compared. However, there were some differences with respect to starting times. Those who had experienced starting times before 7.00 a.m. were less likely to express an intention to continue their education after school but more likely to admit having had work-related absence from school.

TABLE 5.10 Start and finish times and commitment to education.

		Early start	Late finish
1	Returned to S5	ns	ns
2	Not truanted	ns	ns
3	Plans continued education	*	ns
4	Attendance	ns	ns
5^	Not missed school to work	**	ns
6^	Not off school after work	**	ns
7^	Not missed class after work	**	ns

Statistic: Chi squared
^ Applies to only to students with experience of work.
* $p < .05$.
** $p < .01$.
ns p value not significant.
Note: All of the significant relationships were negative.

Given the limited nature of the data on starting and finishing times, these results should be regarded as indicating that it would be worth while exploring the effects of early starting employing more precise measures.

So far we have not distinguished between schools and regions in our analysis. There were no significant differences between the rural and urban schools in the extent of student employment. However, there were some differences in commitment to education and academic performance. Significant differences between the schools were found in three 'commitment to education' variables, attendance, admitting to truanting and returning to school in S5. When the regions were compared, only two variables showed significant variations, pupils in the rural schools having the better attendance rates and admitting to truancy less. It is worth noting that the rural schools had smaller school populations than the urban schools. It may be that differences in attendance rates and truanting reflects the ease of monitoring pupils in small schools. Significant differences in academic performance were also found when schools were compared. However, when the schools were grouped by region, there was no significant difference between the urban and the rural pupils. This would suggest that the links between employment and schooling reported earlier may transcend the rural–urban divide.

To test the hypothesis that working was more likely to be found in schools with greater levels of poverty, schools were ranked on the basis of the proportion of pupils receiving free school meals and the proportion receiving clothing grants. The schools were also ranked on the proportion of pupils in the sample who were currently working and also on the proportion who had ever worked. Employing Spearman's Rank Order Correlation (Rho), we found no support for the hypothesis. Indeed the only significant relationship suggests the reverse, in that schools with the higher proportions of clothing grants tend to have lower proportions of pupils who have ever worked.

Schools were again ranked in order of the percentage of pupils in receipt of free school meals and clothing grants. In addition the various measures of commitment to education were ranked. There was no evidence to support the general hypothesis that poverty influences the degree of commitment to education. However, one significant result to emerge suggests a positive relationship between the proportion of pupils in receipt of free school meals and the number of pupils who admitted truanting from school. Those schools with the greater proportion of pupils receiving clothing grants also had higher numbers of pupils reporting having truanted.

What can be concluded from this study? We tested four basic hypotheses:

1. Pupils who work show a weaker commitment to education than those who do not work.
2. Pupils who work have a poorer level of academic performance than those who do not work.
3. Pupils who work longer hours show a weaker commitment to education than those who work shorter hours.
4. Pupils who work longer hours have a poorer level of academic performance than those who work shorter hours.

Broadly speaking the evidence does *not* support the hypotheses that those who work will perform less well and show less commitment to education. However when the workers are subdivided with respect to hours worked, we found that those who worked longest (over 10 hours per week) tend to perform less well and show less commitment to education.

Our results do not allow us to draw firm conclusions about differences between rural and urban areas. On the other hand, a rather simpler point can be made, namely that schools can differ in the character of the work its pupils undertake and the impact of that work on schooling. For example, whereas typically almost 9 out of 10 working pupils have never had a work permit, in one of the schools studied more than half of those who had worked had had a permit. This appeared to stem from that school's policy of making pupils aware of the need for permits. In other cases, variations in the jobs undertaken seemed linked to the nature of the local economy.

THIRD STUDY: CUMBRIA

We can now turn to the educational data collected in the Cumbrian investigations which we reported in Chapter 4. The measures of educational performance used were based on the GCSE results achieved by individual students. As with Standard Grade performance in the Scottish study, examining performance on individual GCSE subjects was felt to be of limited value given that the range of options available differed between schools. As with the Scottish students, for ease of analysis we decided to standardize the measure of performance in the form of a score for each student. GCSE grades ranged from A (highest) to G (lowest). These were converted to a global score for each student on the following basis, Grade A = 7, Grade B = 6, and so on. A student's scores in the various subjects assessed were then combined.

Commitment to education was assessed on the basis of the same objective measures as in Scotland, Attendance and Progression (to Year 12). In the case of one school, entry to a Sixth Form College was the appropriate criterion.

As Table 5.11 indicates, students who had never worked performed significantly better than current or former workers. However, it is worth noting that current workers achieved a higher score, on average, than those students who were former workers.

An analysis of Year 11 attendance records found that students' work status was significantly related to attendance at school. Students who had never worked had better attendance rates than current and former workers.

Examining the relationship between work status and progression to Year 12 it was found that former workers were the least likely group to return to school

TABLE 5.11 Work and academic performance.

Employment status	N[a]	Mean score
Current worker	226	30
Former worker	129	25
Never worked	89	32

[a] N: number of students in each category.

TABLE 5.12 Work and attendance.

	N[a]	Mean attendance (%)
Current worker	228	88
Former worker	133	88
Never worked	88	92

[a] N: number of students in each category.

TABLE 5.13 Work and return to Year 12.

	N[a]	Return to year 12 (%)
Current worker	82	35
Former worker	33	24
Never worked	39	42

[a] N: number of students in each category.

after completing Year 11. The students most likely to return to school were those in the never worked category.

We saw that, in the second Scottish study, educational commitment and performance were related to hours worked. The questionnaire completed by Year 11 students in Cumbria did not address term-time working hours. However, as we demonstrated earlier there is a correlation between the hours worked in Year 10 and hours worked over the school holidays. It seemed worth looking at the working hours students had reported in Year 10 and relating those to educational variables.

The figures in Table 5.14 clearly mirror those of the second Scottish study. An analysis of the hours worked in Year 10 in relation to progression to Year 12 demonstrated that students working over 10 hours per week were significantly less likely to have stayed on to Year 12.

TABLE 5.14 Hours worked and performance.

	N[a]	Mean score
Low hours (up to 5)	77	33
Moderate hours (6–10)	77	30
High hours (over 10)	41	21

[a] N: number of students in each category.

One of the advantages of the Cumbrian study was that it allowed us to follow students over a longer period of time than either of the Scottish studies. Taking into consideration the information gathered from both the Year 10 and Year 11 surveys enabled us to examine students' movement in and out of employment.

Four categories were created which took account of whether a student had *ever worked* in Year 10 and employment status at the time of completing a questionnaire in Year 11:
1. Consistent worker: employed in Years 10 and 11.
2. Not working in Year 11 having been working in Year 10.
3. Working in Year 11 having not been working in Year 10.
4. Consistent non-worker: not employed in Years 10 and 11.

This allows us to explore whether moving in and out of work at these stages is related to educational commitment or performance.

TABLE 5.15 Work status.

	N^a	(%)
1. Consistent worker	191	43
2. Stopped working In Y11	129	29
3. Started working In Y11	18	4
4. Consistent non-worker	103	23

[a] N: number of students in each category.

Almost two-thirds of the students are consistently either workers or non-workers by this stage in their schooling. It is more common for students to stop working in Year 11 than to start working then for the first time. This suggests that most of those who had not been working in Year 10 were firmly committed to not having a job before GCSE examinations. On the other hand a high proportion of those working in Year 10, gave up working by Year 11. One reason might have been approaching examinations.

If we compare the educational performance of students in these categories, differences in mean GCSE score are statistically significant.

TABLE 5.16 Work status and performance.

	Mean score
1. Consistent worker	30
2. Stopped working in Y11	24
3. Started working in Y11	37
4. Consistent non-worker	32

Students who started working in Year 11 achieved the highest mean score, but it is worth pointing out the very small number of students in this category. However, analysis of the data found that the key difference between the groups in relation to GCSE score was that students who had *stopped* working in Year 11 had significantly poorer scores than the other three categories. If students stopping work in Year 11 did indeed do so because of anxieties about their

TABLE 5.17 Work status and attendance.

	Mean attendance (%)
1. Consistent worker	88
2. Stopped working in Y11	87
3. Started working in Y11	88
4. Consistent non-worker	92

forthcoming examination performance, then it appears not to have had the intended results.

Using the complete attendance records for Year 11 as a measure of commitment to schooling, the following results (as shown in Table 5.17) were found. Note that consistent non-workers had the highest average attendance. The others did not differ significantly among themselves.

Students in the original Year 10 study were asked whether they intended continuing in education beyond secondary schooling. It was found that both consistent and non-consistent workers were those most likely to have expressed an intention to continue in education. When Year 12 records were examined, it was found that students who had worked in both Year 10 and Year 11 and those who had never worked were most likely to have actually progressed to Year 12. This suggests a degree of consistency between stated commitment in Year 10 to continuing education and actually staying on at school.

IMPLICATIONS

Our three studies covered students in 12 schools which are not necessarily representative of the country as a whole. This should be kept in mind when considering what conclusions can be drawn from our results. Whenever we cite any of our findings in support of an argument, a phrase such as 'if our results are confirmed by further studies' should be assumed.

One conclusion which our research would support is that the relation between employment and schooling is something which is worth considering in its own right. The fact that child labour world wide is clearly associated with poverty leads some people to assume that child employment in Britain is driven by poverty. Anyone adopting this point of view might assume that since child workers will come mainly from families of low socio-economic status, to compare children who work with children who do not work is essentially to compare social classes. By this point of view, any relations shown between work and education will be mere by-products of social class influences on education. Our results do not support such crude assumptions. There was a slight tendency opposite to that hypothesized by the 'work-because-of poverty' argument. We found a tendency for higher rates of work in less deprived schools. Insofar as differences were found, there seemed marginally fewer workers in schools with high indicators of deprivation.

Let it be noted that it is not our position that, in attempting to understand British child labour, 'Poverty does not matter'. We think it is important to try to study the effects of work on children probably overlooked by our study, those who have largely dropped out of school in favour of work. Such children will be harder to identify and investigate. They are certainly not open to study by the school-centred methods which we have employed. Some of these children, perhaps most of them, may well come from particularly deprived backgrounds, and their problems need to be understood. Although we have not found any evidence for it, some children in Britain may be forced to work out of economic necessity. What we would deny, however, is that these make up the bulk of working children. Many children work without any obvious economic need. This must be taken into account when we try to understand the phenomenon of child employment.

Having argued that the relationship between child labour and schooling is worth studying in its own right, we must now answer an obvious question. What can we claim to have demonstrated? The most basic point which emerges is that, if one wishes to judge child employment by its effect on the child's education, then one cannot condemn part-time jobs out of hand. When one compares workers with non-workers, there is no general tendency for the latter to show up as superior either in terms of actual performance academically or in terms of the commitment shown to schooling. Equally, it cannot be said that our results give much support to the idea that working benefits the child's education, at least as assessed by the criteria we have used.

The message which we believe should be conveyed to parents, policy makers and researchers is that the inter-relationship between part-time employment and schooling is a complex one. A parent worried about the possible detrimental effects on educational achievement who poses the question 'Should I allow my child to have a job?' must at present be met with an answer which is not necessarily welcome: 'It depends on the job.'

What aspects of a job should be considered? In our second study we looked at the number of hours worked, drawing distinctions between up to 5, up 10 and over 10 hours per week. These hours may seem modest and only a very small percentage of child workers appear to breach the legal limits on the working week for school children. However, one must recall that if one wishes to assess the total weekly 'work' of a school student one needs to add hours at school, homework and possibly household chores as well. Keeping that in mind, our findings are not too surprising. A fairly clear tendency exists for the longer hours to be associated with poor performance at, and commitment to, school. Note, too, that we found hours worked related to examination performance in the Cumbrian study as well, even though the information on hours worked had been collected quite a long time before the examinations were sat.

We have already stressed that our results do not demonstrate *causality*. That is a reasonable point for researchers to consider. However, in the face of the evidence, it is surely appropriate that parents should be cautious and seek to limit the hours worked.

Legislation in Britain is clearly based on the assumption that *when* a child works is as important as how *much* work is undertaken. Seven in the morning is the earliest permitted starting time; seven in the evening the legal limit for stopping work. These regulations are widely flouted, especially with regard to evening work. Looking for possible effects on schooling, we found that there was little evidence to show such evening work had detrimental effects. However, starting early in the morning was associated with certain negative indicators of commitment to schooling.

There are obviously many other ways in which work can vary besides hours worked. If we are concerned with possible harmful effects on schooling, there are some likely candidates for investigation, including the physical effort required and amount of responsibility. However, these did not fall within the scope of our studies and must be left for further investigation.

It is possible that some readers may feel that the tone of this discussion so far has been somewhat paternalistic. We picture parents needing to monitor the child's working. But what of the child's perspective? Does the child need protection? Are children capable of assessing, and reacting to, their own needs? The 'snapshot' approach adopted in out first two studies did not provide us with much evidence.

Work should not be seen as something which simply 'happens to' a school student. We should be exploring why they take jobs and why they leave jobs, and, in so doing, we should be taking account of the question of what part educational concerns play in the decisions. Does a feeling of success at school encourage the student to think that it would be 'safe' to take on a part-time job? Does anxiety about poor performance at school lead to some students giving up their jobs? How good are students at judging the influence on their school work of outside factors such as part-time employment? How much pressure do parents and teachers put on students because they see work as potentially harmful to schooling? And how do the student workers respond to such pressure? These are simple questions to ask and, we believe, relevant ones. To attempt an adequate answer to any of them will require much more painstaking research than has been attempted so far.

Although we have made comparisons of current and former workers, students working low and high hours, students starting work, early and late, students finishing early and late, and Cumbrian students starting and leaving work in Year 11, these categories simply summarize certain aspects of the variability of work. The reader may recall here that, when we looked in detail at the individual work histories of some of the Cumbrian students whom we questioned over a period of two years, a considerable variety of different patterns emerged. With the exception of one student who never worked, there was no obvious simple pattern of work history which fitted many of the students. Some started young and continued, others started young then stopped. Pupils moved in and out of jobs quite frequently in some cases. With such variations in working lives, it would require quite detailed investigation to demonstrate those circumstances in which work did and did not harm academic performance and attitudes.

If more thoroughgoing research takes place, then due recognition needs to be given to more optimistic perspectives on child employment. This will involve broadening our conception of what evidence needs to be collected. Optimism applies not just to writers, such as Green (1990), who believe that on the whole students are capable of monitoring the effects of work and responding appropriately. There is also the perspective which views part-time employment as part of the child's long-term career strategy. Work undertaken while still at school, from this point of view, educates the child about some of the realities of the workplace, teaches valuable practical skills and can thus be seen as preparation for the adult job market. In order to check whether this corresponds to reality, we would need to follow students through into early adulthood and discover whether the ex-child workers actually find themselves in better paid and more satisfying jobs than their classmates who did not work while at school. If this were indeed to turn out to be the case, then one would have to acknowledge that for those children their part-time employment contributed to their education. It seems likely that when such investigations do take place, the answer will have the same sort of qualifications as needed to be made when we considered the effect of jobs on school. In other words, 'it depends on the job' will feature as part of the answer.

From time to time, we have alluded to the fact that research on these matters is much more advanced in the United States than in Britain. It would be pleasant to think that American investigators could save their British counterparts a good deal of time and energy. Can we simply infer that clear American results will apply to Britain. Unfortunately, for those who have to fund and carry out research, the answer has to be no. It is not that we can ignore American research. On the contrary, it can provide useful guides. But it can only guide us on what to look for, it cannot guarantee that we will find just what they found. An example will illustrate. Greenberger and Steinberg's (1986) research suggested that total hours worked was a significant variable when considering the effects of work on schooling. This encouraged us to look at hours worked in our studies in Scotland and England. We, too, found that it was a significant variable. However, whereas Steinberg and indeed other American researchers have found 20 hours per week part-time employment to be a key dividing point, in Britain we have found differences below and above 5 hours per week, and below and above 10 hours per week. The tendency seems to be the same in both countries. It would be interesting to speculate on why the harmful effect seems to occur at a lower work level. Do

British schools tend to expect more out of school time to be devoted to homework, for example? However, a more important issue is that, from the point of view of implementing research findings, the 'turning point' is crucial. Whether it be policy makers, teachers or students themselves, there is a big difference between saying that working more than 10 hours should be discouraged and working more than 20 hours should be discouraged.

There is still much to be discovered about the complex interaction between the work and education of British children. However, the start that has been made in the research reported in this chapter has shown up some of the serious concerns that need to be addressed.

Chapter 6

Costs and Benefits

Britain, like many of the industrialized countries, has a specific legislative framework, the purpose of which is to control child employment. The 1933 Act (and the equivalent 1937 Act in Scotland), has two main aspects to it. On the one hand, it lays down central, national regulations on matters such as the age at which a child may take up employment, the hours when a child may and may not work, and the types of jobs a child is prohibited from undertaking. On the other hand, the Act makes local authorities responsible for implementing the legislation and gives them powers to lay down supplementary regulations which take account of local circumstances. Thus local authorities have in the past produced their own lists of unacceptable forms of employment. Equally, they may make allowance for the use of children in specified special circumstances. The most common example of the latter has probably been the provisions made in agricultural areas to permit children to be absent from school to take part in seasonal harvesting.

It must be borne in mind, however, that the evidence we have laid out in Chapter 3, collected by other researchers and ourselves, in various parts of the country, strongly suggests that this legislation is ineffective. Most local authorities in theory use a permit system as their basic method of enforcing the law. We have shown that only a very small proportion of working children have ever had such a permit. The others are employed in breach of the law. We shall look at some of the policy implications of this position in Chapter 7.

For the moment, let us consider the underlying principles on which this Act appears to be based. Three assumptions seem to lie at the heart of this legislation. First, childhood is a period of life in which the individual's main role is to be educated. Second, it is not inherently wrong for children of school age to be allowed to work. Third, there is a need to control children's experience of work. The legislation thus allows for the combination of full-time compulsory education with part-time employment.

What lies behind an acceptance of the possibility of part-time employment? Clearly, one consideration has been that children can be useful. We showed in Chapter 1 how through history employers had pled the case for using children. Children have been particularly employed in the national interest in time of war.

However, it would be wrong to suggest that this is the only reason that school children are given the opportunity to work. There is also a common belief that children may gain from the experience of working in a part-time capacity. Such a view does not ignore the possibility of work being harmful. It is to prevent possible harm that the regulation on children's work is aimed.

Over the last decade there has been a growing debate about the potential benefits which children may gain from their work. It is understandable that, at an international level, discussions of child labour have focused on economically underdeveloped countries, where it is much easier to identify the costs of children working than the benefits. This has tended to distract attention from the rather different situation in industrialized countries, where the benefits as well as costs of children working need to be taken seriously. The development of a fuller understanding of the cost and benefit debate was given considerable impetus by the seminal work, *When teenagers work: The psychological and social costs of adolescent employment* (Greenberger and Steinberg, 1986). On the basis of their research programme based in California, Ellen Greenberger and Laurence Steinberg have adopted a critical stance. They suggest that it is necessary to balance such notions that 'work is good' with a willingness to confront the potential that work has to be harmful.

Marsh (1991) suggests that two opposing perspectives have emerged in the child employment literature, the zero sum model and the developmental model. The zero sum model emphasizes the negative impact part-time employment will have on a range of mainly academic outcomes. The reason for this is that given the limited time available to a child's activities, the more time spent on non-academic tasks then the less time there is available for academic pursuits. This idea of a trade-off in time has evolved to include what Marsh calls 'social psychological constructs', such as commitment to school or investment in school. Researchers adopting this model would consider, for example, the amount of time spent in work and its impact in mediating the negative consequences. However, time is not the sole concern, it may also be the case that involvement in work, and the attitudes fostered by it, may be incompatible with the aims and objectives of school.

The alternative approach, the developmental model, according to Marsh, views work as 'character-building'. In this model, part-time work is something to be encouraged during adolescence since it facilitates the transmission of knowledge, the attainment of skills, encourages responsibility and develops an adult perspective. This model adopts a wider view that work experience can develop a range of abilities which, on the surface, are non-academic but which may have positive consequences for specific school tasks. This approach views work as a set of experiences which can contribute to the development of the individual. This model reflects many of the 'commonsense assumptions' which are made by many people in Britain when they start to think about children's part-time work. But what of the research evidence? Does it offer support for one or other of these models?

RESEARCH EVIDENCE

Although the main aim of this book is to consider work by children in British schools, most of the 'costs-and-benefits' evidence available comes from the United States. Nevertheless, it is worth looking at the evidence which Greenberger, Steinberg and others have collected which bears on the issue of how work can be 'good' and 'bad' for adolescents. We shall consider it now, keeping in mind that research findings will not necessarily always be mirrored on this side of the Atlantic.

Cultural differences may be of significance. For example, in the United States, the trend to mix education and work among university and college students has been established for some time. 'Working your way through college' is a well-established aspect of higher education, partly reflecting the funding arrangements for college and universities. This may filter down through the system to influence the attitudes of children in high school towards mixing part-time work and education.

Second, American researchers use a different definition of children in their studies. While our studies have adopted our country's legal concept of a child as anyone under 16 years of age, the American studies include adolescents up to the age of 18 years. (This is in line with the United Nations Convention on the Rights of the Child.) It may be that conclusions drawn from such studies are not necessarily applicable to a younger population.

Even with these caveats, however, it is our opinion that the American studies have shed important light on to the debate about the impact of part-time employment.

The zero sum model assumes that the debate regarding the benefits and costs of part-time work should take place in the education arena. In other words, the outcome of work should be assessed in terms of the educational attainments of the school students concerned. One of the clearest conclusions to be drawn, if one adopts that perspective, is that little difference emerges if one attempts simply to compare workers and non-workers. American research indicates that the issue is not whether an individual works or not, but rather the number of hours committed to work. As early as 1983, Greenberger was able to argue before a US Congressional committee that children who commit a large amount of their time to work do not do as well academically or show as strong a commitment to education. (See also Greenberger and Steinberg, 1986; Mortimer et al., 1996; Bachman and Schulenberg, 1993; Steinberg and Dornbusch, 1991). Our research reported in Chapter 5 suggests that this is one finding which probably does cross the Atlantic intact.

However what exactly can we conclude from the negative relationship demonstrated between total hours worked and schooling? The data in the previous chapter indicated that working a small number of hours is positively associated with academic performance when compared to those who have never worked. This opens up the question of what precisely it is about work which could help academic performance.

It could be argued that school students gain experiences from work which have an impact on their development and leads to the acquisition of skills which are transferable from work to school. It is also possible that school skills are reinforced in the world of work. Greenberger (1983) was able to show that children who work had better performance on tests of practical knowledge, including topics such as business and economic and consumer affairs.

Experience of employment may also have a positive impact on the individual's social–cognitive development. Steinberg et al. (1981a) showed that working adolescents had a greater understanding of social relationships and were better able to accommodate themselves to other people's roles and views. In addition they showed a higher sensitivity to the moods and temperament of others.

Vygotsky's model, which is enjoying a revival of interest among developmental psychologists at present, could provide a theoretical base from which to explore this idea further. Vygotsky's theory treats cognitive development as being influenced by our social and cultural experiences (Newman and Holzman, 1993). If this is the case, then employment could be a type of social experience which introduces the individual to new modes of thought.

Saxe (1988), in a study of Brazilian street vendors aged 10 to 12 years of age, found evidence which illustrates the impact of cultural experience on cognitive development. The children in the study had little or no schooling, yet Saxe was able to show that their everyday experiences provided them with the capacity to solve mathematical problems. The results are interpreted as supporting the view that the children had constructed novel understandings based upon the problems they are faced with in their employment. Such levels of understanding were not available to non-workers.

It would be interesting to consider the extent to which such conclusions could be transferred to countries such as Britain and the United States. It is possible that part-time work enhances cognitive abilities by allowing the child to construct new levels of understanding or it may simply reinforce knowledge already attained from within the school system. As yet we are not aware of any research which has considered the impact of work in Britain from this perspective.

It may be that research so far has taken too narrow a view of attainments, assessing them largely as they are normally interpreted within the confines of the academic arena. To fully test the developmental model noted by Marsh (1991) may imply that to properly assess the benefits of work we must move beyond the school gate.

AUTONOMY

One aspect of the case for child employment based on the developmental model is the view that part-time work during adolescence will encourage the attainment of autonomy. This is compatible with some of the currently dominant theoretical analyses of adolescence as a period of development. Theorists such as Erikson (1968) have suggested that the adolescent by resolving their own identity will, by implication, become more autonomous. A number of writers stress the need for adolescents to establish their autonomy. It is worth noting that not all researchers clearly define 'autonomy' and in some cases use the term independence as a synonym.

By entering part-time employment the individual may be taking one of the first tentative steps towards independence in a number of ways, namely choosing a job, applying for it, being interviewed. Cole (1980) has suggested that in this way the individual can acquire important skills, such as how to identify jobs, how to keep the job once you have got it, how to organize your time and how to manage money. Successfully achieving these goals could be significant elements in establishing one's independence from others, especially one's parents.

Finch et al. (1991) have linked the individual's part-time work experience with his or her sense of control. The extent to which we feel in charge of what is happening (internal locus of control) or lacking influence on what is happening (external locus of control) are perceived as relevant to a range of psychological variables. Finch and his colleagues conclude from their research investigations that work experience exerts an influence on mastery orientation. They found that internal mastery was highest in those males who perceived their work as being able to provide some long-term opportunities for them, while females had higher internal orientation when their pay levels were judged to be good. Thus, for Finch the relationship between part-time work and sense of internal or external control will be determined by the specific nature of the work experience rather than by such general factors as formal work status or time devoted to the job.

Steinberg et al. (1982a) found that part-time employment encouraged the development of a sense of personal responsibility. Such gains in responsibility were apparent in terms of punctuality, dependability, self-reliance and orientation towards work. However, the study also notes that such gains were greater for females than males. One possible hypothesis to explain this difference lies, in the types of jobs done by males and females. In Chapter 3 we drew attention to the extent to which sex differences existed in terms of part-time work undertaken. It may be that the different forms of employment open to males and females could account for the finding by Steinberg and his colleagues. Alternatively, it could be argued that rather than any intrinsic differences in the job demands between male and females the results may reflect a difference in the interpretation of the work experience between the sexes (Greenberger, 1988).

More recently Steinberg and Dornbusch (1991) have argued that the link between part-time work and the development of psycho-social functioning is rather modest, except in so far as work benefits the individual's sense of self-esteem. Steinberg and Dornbusch take a distinctive position on the issue of autonomy. They define autonomy in terms of the amount of parental control. Their results support the hypothesis that those adolescents who work have a higher degree of independence from parents compared to those who do not work. They suggest that this may arise from two sorts of factors. The independence may be essentially financial in character because of the adolescent's control over his or her earnings. Alternatively, it may be that work necessarily removes the adolescent from contact with his or her parents over certain periods of time and that creates a need for the young worker to exercise autonomy. Steinberg and Dornbusch (1991) do not necessarily view this as a positive process and suggest that it may undermine parental authority in some potentially harmful ways.

On the issue of the financial independence that earned income may provide, Cole (1980), too, notes that monetary reward gained from work provides a degree of independence since adolescents no longer have to rely upon their parents subsidizing them by providing pocket money.

Researchers have also noted that in some cases the money earned may contribute directly to the family budget (see, for example, Pond and Searle, 1991; Manning, 1990; Mortimer and Shanahan, 1994). However, most researchers stress that this is found in a small percentage of cases. We would argue that all adolescents who work contribute indirectly to the family budget through a process of substitution. The young workers may not necessarily see themselves as contributing to a family budget. Nevertheless, products which they buy with their own earnings may very well include items which would come from the family budget if they had not been working. It may be very difficult to tell in practice which of an adolescent worker's purchases are made solely because he or she has an independent income and which would have been bought irrespective of whether that additional source of income existed.

Should we assume that part-time earnings increase autonomy? Cole (1980) suggests that the degree of autonomy attained is limited, with parents exerting some degree of control or monitoring of expenditure. Manning (1990) supports this view arguing that, the higher the earnings, the more parents increased their attempts to control spending patterns. Manning indicates that this may lead to increased disagreements between adolescent workers and their parents.

Since we cannot be sure of the outcome of such disputes, we should not assume that earnings from part-time work necessarily leads to autonomous decision-making. However, recent work by Aronson et al. (1996) has highlighted the fact that adolescents who work perceive that they gain an awareness of money management from their part-time work. Self-perceptions may provide an important insight into the actual impact of the work experience of adolescents. It may be the case that what matters is that the adolescents themselves see their earnings from work as a source of a sense of autonomy and allows them to feel that they are developing money management skills.

Yet, it can be doubted whether having a substantial independent income necessarily leads to greater ability to handle money wisely. Bachman (1983) has raised an important concern regarding the earning power of children who work. It is his contention that while they may be earning money they are not gaining a realistic appreciation of the value of earned income. Bachman argues that adolescents may experience 'premature affluence'. The situation which he envisages as problematic is a combination of relatively high income levels and parents permitting the young workers to treat this as discretionary spending money. Bachman argues that if parents are still meeting the costs of living expenses, adolescents do not learn important lessons about apportioning income between their immediate desires and longer term needs, such as housing. Bachman does not provide substantial evidence on how common or uncommon the scenario he outlines might be. Nevertheless his argument provides us with a useful reminder that it is too simplistic to assume that having a job leads automatically to 'good' monetary education.

FAMILY AND PEERS

A major concern inherent in the zero sum model is that part-time employment encroaches upon a valuable but scarce resource: time. Hours spent in a job may be hours which might be more valuably spent elsewhere. One area from which time may be lost is in contact with the family.

Family relations during adolescence has long attracted the attention of psychologists interested in development (see, for example, Noller and Callan, 1991). Research has indicated that children who work do spend less time with their families (Cole, 1980; Greenberger et al., 1980). However, we need to be cautious and not jump to the conclusion that quantity of contact is necessarily linked to quality of contact. This is an issue of which researchers in attachment relations have been aware for some time (cf. Sylva and Lunt, 1985).

As we have already noted, some studies do argue that part-time employment does remove the individual from important parental contact (Steinberg and Dornbusch, 1991). Greenberger and Steinberg (1986) had previously argued that part-time work reduced opportunities for contact such as shared family meals. Manning (1990) has focused specifically on the quality of relationships between working adolescents and parents. She argues that work may compromise these relations in a number of areas. Adolescents who worked were found to have more disagreements with their parents about helping around the house, about staying out late, about smoking, about drinking and drug use, about money, about school, and about getting along with the family. Manning also argued that parents were less likely to monitor the activities of working adolescents as compared to nonworking adolescents. Restrictions on television-watching and supervision of homework were two areas where differences emerged between how parents tended to treat workers and non-workers. In addition, those adolescents who worked were less likely to have to let their parents know where they were and had later curfew times on schooldays.

In interpreting these findings, Manning believes it is possible to argue that work may foster levels of independence in adolescents with which parents may be uncomfortable, thus increasing discord within the family.

Mortimer and Shanahan (1994) found that intensity of work experience was related to the feelings of male adolescents that they had become more independent from the family. They believe they spent less time with the family unit and that arguments emerged with parents around the issue of work. For females that pattern was less clear but there were indications that work intensity led them to perceive that family time was limited and led to arguments with parents.

Such findings are in line with Greenberger and Steinberg's (1986) negative interpretation of the impact of work on family relations. Mortimer and Shanahan (1994) do not wish to uncritically endorse this negative interpretation, however. Instead they argue that we need to look at the results in the context of adolescent–parent normative developmental patterns. Separation from parents is part of this stage of life. Because of this, we should expect time spent with parents will diminish. On this analysis, working simply accentuates a process which is already occurring. What is important for Mortimer and Shanahan is that they believe their results show no qualitative differences in parent–adolescent relations when looking at workers and non-workers. In fact they argue that the work experience may have positive consequences for the family, particularly with respect to father–son relations.

This may emerge if male adolescents perceive their work as adding to their skills and moving them towards adulthood. Parents, in turn, view this in a positive light and perceive changes in their offspring as beneficial, hence potentially contributing to good relationships between father and son. This pattern of results was not found for females who worked and may reflect differential expectations of parents for their male and female children.

Recently Call (1996) has drawn attention to the functional role of work for adolescents in dealing with family disruption. Call suggests that work may act as a supportive framework for adolescents dealing with stress at home. There is an important caveat to be noted, in that Call is talking about specific types of adolescent work. Work which is satisfying and engaging is deemed to be able to provide some support by acting as a form of distraction from the problems at home. In addition, work experience which offers social support and increases coping skills will make a positive contribution to the individual's capacity to deal with life challenges. As we shall see later, there is a debate about how extensive such forms of work experience are in practice in the children's labour market.

Call (1996) is emphasizing an important point. Researchers who focus on social support systems need to consider work as a possible source of such support during adolescence. Traditionally the focus has tended to be on the adolescents peer group. Since child employment has now been demonstrated to be such a widespread phenomenon, it is difficult for researchers into social support systems to ignore work as a potentially significant factor.

Given the concerns over the impact of work on family relations it is surely natural to raise the issue of the potential effect of employment on peer relations. However, this is a subject which has not received a great deal of empirical investigation. Studies by Greenberger et al. (1980) and Steinberg et al. (1982a) agree that working has little or no effect on the amount of time spent with peers or with the quality of the relationships. Greenberger and her colleagues do note that those who have part-time jobs are more likely to be involved with friends of the opposite sex. It is suggested that this may reflect an increased contact with opposite sex peers in the workplace.

It seems to us surprising that the impact of work on peer relations has been relatively neglected. There is some indication that work may have qualitative effects on peer relations. Steinberg et al. (1982a) found that emotional closeness with peers declined with increasing time spent at work. Perhaps a more fruitful line of enquiry would be to consider the impact of part-time work on the individual's status within the peer group or the way that part-time employment may re-structure peer contacts. Phillips and Sandstrom (1990) have indicated that there is some status effect associated with working. From our own anecdotal information, we would anticipate that this may not only be related to whether you work but the type of job that is done as well.

FUTURE EMPLOYMENT

One of the central commonsense assumptions to be found underlying the 'work is good' viewpoint is that there is some relationship between children's part-time work experience and adult roles in the world of work. This could encompass both the acquisition of skills relevant to work and the development of attitudes to work which prove helpful in later life.

That early work experience may be advantageous is a position espoused by economists such as Meyer and Wise (1982, cited in Mortimer and Finch, 1986). Their studies indicated that adolescents who had part-time jobs were more likely to gain employment after the completion of their education. In addition, the hourly earnings of those who have substantial work experience in adolescence may be higher than those with limited work experience or no experience of work at all.

Greenberger (1988) argues that such findings need to be viewed from both a short-term and long-term perspective. In her opinion, the gains which can be demonstrated for those with part-time work experience may be in the short term only. The effects of having had work experience may be much less significant overall than the fact that, in general, individuals with more schooling and higher qualifications achieve greater long-term labour-market success as indicated by salary level, job type and job satisfaction.

Greenberger's concern is that evidence indicates that working while at school, particularly excessive levels of work, has a depressive effect on grades, attainment and intention to remain in school. Thus she argues that when school students devote substantial amounts of time to work they are in effect reducing their chances of long-term success in the labour market.

Such views are echoed by Mortimer and Finch (1986). They believe that long-term perspectives need to be adopted by policy makers in this area. They state that:

> The student who becomes highly involved in work while still in high school acquires weaker academic credentials. Given that there are not enough jobs in the primary labor market to go around, his chances in the competition for the higher paying, more secure, and career like employments is therefore reduced.
> (Mortimer and Finch, 1986: 87)

Greenberger (1988) makes the telling point that very few adolescents who work actually stay in that form of employment when they enter the adult labour force. Here Greenberger is questioning the implicit assumption that there is a natural continuity between the types of jobs carried out by people when they are adolescents and those they do when they become adults. From the evidence which she and her colleagues have collected, we can say that the majority of children are employed in jobs which are repetitive, which require low levels of skill and which are widely regarded as menial (see Greenberger and Steinberg, 1986). In such circumstances, it can be argued adolescents may develop attitudes and values towards work which are less than positive. To equate early work experience with positive occupational socialization is too simplistic. It would not be surprising if many of the school students who undertake poorly paid, low status, intrinsically uninteresting jobs may in fact develop what Steinberg et al. (1981b) termed 'occupational cynicism'. This manifests itself in negative attitudes towards work, such as not going 'beyond the call of duty'.

Greenberger and Steinberg (1986) have further argued that extrinsic occupational rewards, rather than intrinsic rewards, come to dominate. Work becomes associated with earning money, which can in turn be used to purchase goods. Such attitudes may be linked to Bachman's (1983) concerns about 'premature affluence'.

Such a pessimistic picture is not painted by all researchers. For example, Stern et al. (1990) found that there was a link between the quality of the employment experience and levels of motivation. Jobs which provided the individual with the potential to learn and which provided some challenge were related to higher degrees of motivation in general. Work which made use of school students' skills were less likely to contribute to cynical attitudes about employment.

Other studies have highlighted the possibility that the experience of part-time employment on future employment and work orientation may differ significantly between male and female school students. Stevens et al. (1992) found such a differential effect of employment on male and female students. Work for males was viewed as a traditionalizing influence, in that it tended to develop a future orientation towards family life, family size and expectations of being the sole breadwinner. For females, work experience lessened commitment to traditional roles.

Stevens and his colleagues place emphasis on the fact that we need to remember the broader picture when considering the role of employment in adolescence. As Steinberg et al. (1981b) note, variables such as sex and social class are crucial in terms of long-term occupational development. Bearing in mind such factors, part-time work may only be a minor influence on an individual's career opportunities. That is not a reason for neglecting the role of work entirely in what must be treated as a complex process.

BEHAVIOURAL EFFECTS

Greenberger (1983) argues that, in evaluating the impact of part-time employment on adolescents, it is necessary to consider its effect on a wide range of behaviours. For example, she indicates that research shows that work is associated with an increase in the use of cigarettes, alcohol and marijuana. Support for this view comes from Steinberg et al. (1982a) and Steinberg and Dornbusch (1991). The latter study takes the argument further by linking long working hours to drug and alcohol use, higher rates of delinquency and levels of psychosomatic distress. How are we to explain such results? Steinberg and Dornbusch (1991) propose three alternative explanations:

1. that increased discretionary income is used to engage in deviant and illegal behaviours, which then cause distress;
2. that work causes stress and the outcomes observed can be regarded as evidence of the form of coping strategies used;
3. that workers have contact with older adolescents and with adults and it is through these contacts that they are exposed to illicit activities.

Some might find the second hypothesis rather perplexing, as the idea of adolescents suffering from work stress is not a familiar one in our society. However, on reflection one may find a number of ways in which adolescent stress might arise through work. First, stress may arise from characteristics of the job itself, for example, pressure to meet production targets. Second, stress may be due to particular types of experience at work such as bad relationships with colleagues or one's boss. Third, stress might emerge from attempts to balance the competing demands of job, school, family and friends.

The impact of such stress can manifest itself in terms of depressive affect (see Shanahan et al., 1991; Mortimer et al., 1992), although some of these studies have only found this effect in males. Both of the cited studies argue that it is the characteristics of the job which are likely to be the most important mediating variable.

Recently Mortimer et al. (1996) have suggested that, while they find it difficult to support the view that working will always be deleterious in its effects, they do find compelling evidence to demonstrate the link between alcohol consumption and employment. Their study thus reinforced earlier evidence of the link between work intensity and alcohol use (see Greenberger and Steinberg, 1986; Steinberg and Dornbusch, 1991; Steinberg et al., 1993). While Mortimer et al. provide evidence of the relationship, they believe that no clear explanation currently exists for this pattern. In other words, they do not find it possible to decide whether any of the hypotheses Steinberg and Dornbusch outlined above can be seen as the strongest.

This finding on alcohol consumption seems to be the most widely acknowledged behavioural correlate of teenage working among researchers. Other findings are less clear cut, which suggests that the potential effect of employment on adolescents' behaviour needs to be much more carefully scrutinized by researchers. We appear ready to accept that work can have a wide range of effects on adults and spend considerable research resources investigating these. In doing so we implicitly accept that work and mental health are related. Should we be surprised that this relationship may also apply to children who work?

This general discussion of the costs and benefits of employment could be extended to include some issues that have already been touched upon. For example, in Chapter 3, we drew attention to the potential health and safety problems associated with employment. Such an issue would obviously be relevant to any evaluation of whether work is 'good' or 'bad'.

We might also want to consider in this context the evidence on gender differentiation in employment. Our results are in line with American findings, in that we found a good deal of difference between boys and girls in the jobs they typically hold. This, too, can be considered relevant to debates about the costs and benefits of employment. If girls while at school do different jobs from their male colleagues is that perhaps contributing to the acceptance of traditional differentiation in adult jobs. It might be argued that adolescent work is perpetuating sex role distinctions in society at large. However, the issue is likely to be a complex one since, as we have seen, there is some evidence which indicates that females with part-time work may develop higher levels of autonomy and non-traditional role expectation (Stevens et al., 1992).

What the discussion has shown up until this point is that there is no unequivocal answer to whether work is 'good' or 'bad' for children. Greenberger and Steinberg

(1986) have described the situation as involving a 'delicate balance' between the costs and benefits. We find this metaphor a telling one. If such an interpretation is accepted, we might want to ask what are the forces which influence the 'balance'?

THE BALANCE BETWEEN COSTS AND BENEFITS

If we adopt Greenberger and Steinberg's (1986) idea of a 'balance' then at the very least we would want to maintain some equilibrium between the costs and benefits. More optimistically, we might wish to set out to create an imbalance to the extent that we can maximize the potential benefits and minimize the potential costs.

Adopting such an approach would lead us towards identifying those variables which seem to exert the greatest influence on the beneficial and harmful impact of employment. In the research two key variables have been identified as warranting attention. These are the number of hours worked and the form of work undertaken.

HOURS WORKED

For a number of years, Greenberger, Steinberg and a number of their colleagues have argued that work intensity is the most important variable. Work intensity is generally assessed by the number of hours typically worked in a week. We have already noted the potential role of work intensity in the context of the education debate in the previous chapter.

A number of studies have identified the relationship between committing an excessive number of hours to work (15 to 20 hours) during term time and a number of problems including lower academic achievement (D'Amico, 1984; Mortimer and Finch, 1986; Steinberg et al., 1982a), higher rates of alcohol and drug use (Greenberger et al., 1981; Steinberg and Dornbusch, 1991; Steinberg et al., 1982a; Mortimer et al., 1996), diminished parental supervision (Greenberger and Steinberg, 1986; Steinberg and Dornbusch, 1991) greater psychological distress and somatic complaints (Greenberger and Steinberg, 1986; Steinberg and Dornbusch, 1991).

To minimize these negative consequences then there needs to be adequate control over the number of hours worked. As yet there is no agreement as to what the optimum number of hours may be. An additional problem would be how far it would be possible to generalize such a 'watershed' prescription across cultures. We have already noted our own finding which indicates the negative consequence of work emerged for those in Britain working in excess of 10 hours a week. Research in the United States suggests that work must last a good deal longer before negative effects can be clearly shown. It is unrealistic to expect that some specific transcultural number of hours will be identified.

We also need to be cautious in assuming that a linear relationship lies at the heart of this relationship. Bachman and Schulenberg (1993) for example note that:

> By far the most dominant finding was that with each increase in the number of hours worked the associated problems also increased. It is also the case that no work at all is not necessarily better than 1–5 hours of work per week.
>
> (Bachman and Schulenberg, 1993: 231)

Based on such data we would be wrong to assume that zero hours of work is the simple end point of any continuum which seeks to establish the degree of benefit of working hours. There is some overlap between these findings and research on the relationship between education and hours worked. Mortimer et al. (1996) have suggested that working a small number of hours may be of some potential benefit. This is of course in line with our own findings in Scotland and England.

If further research confirms this tendency for those working only a little to show some benefit from their employment experience, then two further questions emerge. First, does this employment have to take place during school term time or can the benefits be accrued during vacation periods? Second, does it matter when these hours are worked? We are unaware of any research that has focused on comparing the impact of summer vacation work versus term-time work. Lacking any hard evidence, we may risk the speculation that holidays jobs are less likely to have any sort of damaging effects on educational development than jobs done during term time. In contrast we see no reason to expect either holiday or term-time jobs to have any edge as far as benefits are concerned. We would predict, therefore, that on balance vacation employment is preferable.

We have not found any American research which has considered when children work in the day. Perhaps this is a reflection of the fact that most children who work do so after school. However, in Britain we need to take account of the fact that virtually all milk delivery and a good deal of newspaper delivery takes place in the morning before school starts. We have found early starts to be quite common in the areas of Britain we have studied.

In the course of visiting schools around the country, we have come across numerous anecdotal reports which draw attention to the problem of children rising early before school in order to go to work. Some investigation of this is warranted. If it can be identified that a few hours of work a week can produce benefits, when those hours are worked becomes important. We suspect that working say eight hours per week before going to school will turn out not to be the same in its effect as working eight hours a week after school or eight hours a week at weekends.

THE TYPE OF JOB

Some researchers have expressed reservations about analyses which lay a heavy emphasis on exploring the costs and benefits of working for different lengths of time. For example, Mortimer et al. (1996) have questioned the emphasis on work intensity. They consider that the nature of the work undertaken is likely to turn out to be more important on closer inspection.

When people talk about children's jobs in an everyday context or even in political debates, there is often an implicit assumption about the types of jobs children do. The research we have reported in earlier chapters clearly shows that children work in a wide variety of types of jobs, not just the stereotyped 'paper round' (although for children of some ages that is the most common single category of employment).

Having drawn attention to the variety of work done leads us necessarily to ask the question: do the different jobs children actually undertake in Britain today differ in the costs and benefits they bring to those children? On the face of things, these jobs would appear to provide different opportunities and risks, and place different demands on the individuals involved. For example, if it is suggested that children's social skills can be developed from working, then we are inclined to suggest that delivering newspapers at 6.00 a.m. does not provide many opportunities for social discourse. In contrast, it seems reasonable to argue that working in a shop on a Saturday certainly would provide opportunities to develop social skills, particularly if it involved customer interaction as opposed to, say, shelf-stacking.

Greenberger and Steinberg (1986) argued that if one considers the quality of jobs that children work in, one must conclude that the majority tend to be mundane. They neither provide nor require training and are generally perceived as low skill. Having drawn such a conclusion, it is not surprising that these writers highlight the negative consequences of employment.

We need to be cautious about accepting too readily the rather pessimistic viewpoint of Greenberger and Steinberg. It may be necessary to go beyond our casual impressions, as adults, about how demanding or stimulating a particular job may be to a child or adolescent. The evidence which we have presented suggests that delivery jobs are common among younger children but tend to be given up in favour of other types of employment in later years. This could be interpreted as meaning that children, at least to some extent, match the jobs they undertake to their own abilities as they judge them. It may be that Greenberger and Steinberg might have drawn different conclusions if they had paid greater attention to adolescent perceptions of their own jobs. In a recent study in Britain (McKechnie et al., 1996), based on interviews as opposed to the questionnaire employed in the studies we have reported here, the variation of opportunity that jobs offer to adolescents was highlighted. They varied in terms of the level of interaction with adults, the perceived value of the job, the amount of independence or decision-making offered and the individuals' perception of their role in the workplace.

We must acknowledge, however, that in the context of the issue currently under discussion, it is one thing to show that jobs vary, but quite another matter to demonstrate a link between this variation and the potential impact the job has on the individual young worker. Recently researchers have been focusing their attentions upon this variable. In fact, Mortimer et al. (1996) believe that the quality of work experience can be demonstrated to be a significant variable in influencing a range of outcomes.

An example of this role of the quality of work is found in Mortimer et al.'s (1992) study, where they established that when employment is perceived by adolescents as providing them with skills for the future, then the workers concerned gain psychological benefits from the work experience. Work which creates high levels of stress is more likely to lead to negative outcomes in terms of mental health. The same holds true where there is a tension between the demands of school and the demands of work.

Such a viewpoint is endorsed by Finch et al. (1991), where, in the context of developing control orientation in adolescence, the quality of work was found to be more influential to outcome than either work status or work intensity.

Stern et al. (1990) focused on the impact of the quality of work experience to future orientations. The results from this study suggest once again the importance of the type of job. In this case 'quality' of work was assessed by examining a number of features of the job: the way in which the job used current skills, the extent to which the job developed new skills, the level of stress created by the job, and the level of social interaction within the work environment. Jobs which provide a 'quality' experience had a more positive impact on future orientation towards work.

Clearly such studies strongly suggest that there is little point in trying to generalize about all juvenile employment. Jobs vary significantly in a number of ways and the quality of the work experience during adolescence will affect the balance between the costs and benefits of work. Such studies also provide a challenge to researchers. If we wish to maximize the benefits of employment, then we need to identify those types of jobs that facilitate the attainment of a range of pre-defined characteristics. The challenge is partly related to the issue of how we define these characteristics, or what criteria are used to measure 'quality'. Before leaving the issues of work intensity and work quality there is one final point to be made. We have been considering them as isolated variables but what about the possible interaction between these two variables? To take a pair of concrete example. A particular job may be judged to have few positive features, but will that matter if it lasts only an hour a day for five days a week. Another job may be rated as providing a high quality of work. However, can we expect it to be as beneficial to the pupil who works 30 hours per week as to the pupil who works for a more moderate 10 hours per week?

THE CONTEXT OF EMPLOYMENT

We must also accept that the debate about costs and benefits will not be resolved by focusing only on the role of specific variables considered in isolation. Such an approach plays down the importance of the context within which the experience of work is taking place. By referring to the 'context' we are suggesting that the social, developmental and even cultural context will have an impact on the way that the employment experience is interpreted.

Let us try to explain what we mean by this. The population upon which our research has focused are those children under 16 years of age, and more particularly within the 13- to 15-year-old age range. In the United States the population studied by researchers on child labour is usually within the 13- to 18-year-old age range. While the term 'children' is used throughout this book, we are, from a developmental perspective, talking about adolescence.

We have already noted that Marsh (1991) suggested that what he called the developmental model views work as contributing to the 'total development' of the individual. Developmentally, adolescence has to be thought of as a transition stage between childhood and adulthood. This is typified in the work of Erikson (1968) as being a period of identity resolution. Some writers have viewed it as a period of 'storm and stress' (cf. Coleman, 1992). As Coleman and Hendry (1990) point out, however, some writers see this as rather too stark and crude a conceptualization of adolescence. Nevertheless, any theoretical analysis of adolescence has to acknowledge that at this time in their lives people do face a number of what might be termed developmental tasks. One writer lists sexual maturation, career choice, changing family and peer relations as well as the learning required at school among these tasks (Heaven, 1994). Partly due to Erikson's writings, a good deal of emphasis has been placed on something which cuts across these tasks, namely the adolescent establishing his or her own identity and autonomy.

If one focuses on that process, the role of part-time work could be perceived as potentially positive. Coffield et al. (1986) emphasize the role of full-time employment in contributing to this process. Part-time work may also have a role to play. Cole (1980) has suggested that part-time employment introduces adolescents to aspects of the adult world, where work is part of that reality. It may also provide a sense of freedom and awareness of independence for the individual. We have already noted that, to varying degrees, work can lead to some financial independence, a widening of social networks and in some cases the development of new skills.

Such a positive view of employment would be based upon the assumption that there is a harmonious relationship between the tasks adolescents face and the demands of employment. It is also possible to envisage situations where there is a mismatch between these two. For example, just as the transition to secondary school and examination regimes result in demands on time, so too does work demands time. As previously noted, competing demands on time may lead to stress.

Eccles et al. (1993) have discussed concerns about this issue of mismatch, albeit from a somewhat different perspective. It is their contention that a mismatch may emerge between adolescent development and the tasks to be faced and the demands and structures of secondary education. They argue that when a 'lack of fit' exists between the two it will have negative consequences on adjustment to school. This stage-environment model may be applicable to the current debate. The demands of employment may not sit comfortably with the tasks adolescents are facing in the wider environment.

Finch and Mortimer (1985) in a study of the effect of part-time work on education and long-term socio-economic attainment, noted a differential impact related to age. In their study, the negative effect of work manifested itself in lower grades for younger students but not older ones. One could hypothesize that the older student may have been more able to control and balance the competing demands of work and school successfully, while the younger students were unable to do so. For these younger pupils work, rather than contributing to development, may be seen as detrimental.

It has been argued that those who work may develop a 'pseudo-maturity' (Greenberger and Steinberg, 1986, refer to this as pseudo-adulthood), where an individual may have misperceptions of his or her own abilities and status. Bachman and Schulenberg (1993) have argued that work intensity may be related to a 'precocious development syndrome'. However, they are not convinced about the direction of causality, believing that work intensity may be a symptom of such a syndrome rather that a cause. In other words, the precocious adolescent may be more like to heavily commit him- or herself to the job.

Mortimer and Finch (1996) have put forward quite a detailed argument about the work and development relationship. They believe that one can only appraise the balance between costs and benefits if one attends to the meaning and quality of the work experience, and the context in which this is occurring. For example, how the part-time employment is perceived by parents will have an impact on its meaning for the adolescent. Similarly how adolescents' peers view their work will be important to its interpretation.

Mortimer and Finch draw upon Bronfenbrenner's ecological model of development (Bronfenbrenner, 1986). In this model the environment is conceptualized as consisting of four nested systems, moving from the inner micro-system, to the meso-, exo- and macro-systems.

An adolescent's part-time work would be thought of as a micro-system, but this would be one of a number of micro-systems in which the individual would be involved. There is an acknowledgement in the model that these micro-systems interact with each other. For example, the link between part-time work, the school and the home would be perceived as influencing each other. Such interaction constitutes the meso-system level in the model. In moving to the exo-system level, the model takes account of the fact that systems in which the individual does not directly participate may still influence them. The parents' working conditions may affect their views and attitudes towards work, which in turn may affect the adolescent's view of work and his or her attitude to the part-time job. Although the adolescent does not directly experience the parents' working environment, it nevertheless has an indirect effect on the adolescent worker's development.

Finally, there is the macro-system. This final system refers to the ideology, the social institutions, societal structure and culture within which the individual lives. Levels of unemployment, the nature of education and levels of regulation are examples of factors which will affect all other systems in the model.

Bronfenbrenner's argument is that to understand development we need to understand these inter-relationships. In the present context of child employment, the model would imply that if we are to fully understand the impact of employment it is not enough to look at the balance between good and bad and the variables which influence that balance. We need to recognize that what is seen as good or bad will vary across cultures, so that there is no one fixed set of active variables in this balance. The context will define these variables.

Mortimer and Shanahan (1994) considered the interaction between two micro-systems; adolescents' part-time work and the family. The parents view of adolescents' work was positive, since it was seen to make their children more independent. In turn the children perceived themselves as more independent. The fact that both groups viewed work positively meant they were in agreement. In turn that meant that the outcome of the part-time work experience was positive.

It is also possible to see this type of interaction across subcultures. In a comparison of adolescents who worked in rural and urban settings in America, it was found that the context had an impact on the interpretation of the experience (Shanahan et al., 1996). The results of this study indicated that part-time work was interpreted differently in each of the settings. In the rural setting adolescents part-time work is more likely to be seen as adult-like behaviour, since rural work is more likely to be seen as beneficial to the family unit. An example of this is that in the rural setting adolescent earnings are more likely to be spent on the family than on leisure pursuits. In this sense part-time work in the rural setting is interpreted by Shanahan and his colleagues as an integrating force.

These authors go on to argue that this study indicates that the subculture has an impact on the way work is interpreted, not only within the family but also by the adolescent worker. If we can generalize from this, it would suggest that the exo-systems and macro-systems, to use Bronfenbrenner's terminology, may influence the interpretation of work. Such a model would suggest that Greenberger and Steinberg's (1986) focus on the balance between the costs and benefits must be complicated by the fact that the elements within the 'balance equation' may be influenced by wider cultural factors. If a society does not have a compulsory education system, for example, then the impact of work on formal education could not be included in the balance debate. One could still argue that education should be available but it would not be part of the balance problem. Equally at the macro-system level, the view that a society has of childhood will influence the way that the issues of child employment are conceptualized. The outcome is that there would be a different set of variables to be balanced in each culture.

The research and conceptualizations that we have been discussing in this chapter together point to the great complexity which must be inherent in any adequate discussion of child employment. Simple solutions to 'problems' of employment should be viewed with some scepticism, in our view. This applies both to child labour in an individual country such as Britain and to child labour when viewed at a global level. At present there are still more questions than answers in this area.

Chapter 7

SOME CONCLUSIONS

This final chapter has a number of aims. We want first of all to draw some conclusions based upon the data reported in earlier chapters. In doing this a number of issues will be raised. These will include some policy implications of the research in this field. The second aim of the chapter is to consider the current state of research in this area, to suggest where gaps in knowledge exist and to consider some methodological problems which will need to be considered. Third, we shall propose a model for researchers to consider when undertaking future enquiries in this area.

What conclusions can be drawn from the current research? The most obvious place to start is with the number of children who work. We believe we have demonstrated fairly conclusively in Chapter 2 that the research carried out by the present authors and by others indicates that part-time employment is not uncommon amongst children. The overall trend from every study points to the same conclusion: it is the norm for children to have been involved in some form of paid employment before they reach the minimum school-leaving age.

This finding in itself is worthy of attention, simply because it challenges certain common preconceptions. As a society we have taken comfort from the idea that the employment of children is a topic which can be assigned to the history books. When we do talk about child employment in Britain today we do so with reference to economically underdeveloped countries.

This blindness to child employment in Britain has been found, as we have seen, among government ministers, but it is not confined to them. As part of another research project we have recently found ourselves seeking information on the position of British trade unions and non-governmental organizations (NGOs) on the issue of child employment within Britain. The majority have adopted an outward-looking stance, indicating that they saw the problem as one belonging to the developing countries. They had little or nothing to say about the situation in their own country.

There are some exceptions to this picture. The GMB trade union has been active in drawing attention to the issue and recently the Trades Union Congress published data emerging from a survey they had commissioned on child employment, thus indicating that they to are now beginning to consider this as an issue. This latter report simply confirms what is already known about the nature and extent of child employment (Trades Union Congress, 1997) but is nevertheless welcome. Among the NGOs, the Low Pay Unit of London, Manchester and Scotland has been involved in highlighting the issue of child employment. Recently the Save the Children Fund, the Child Poverty Action Group and One World Northern Ireland have begun to become actively involved in publicizing the problems of child workers in their own country. There is a danger in that campaigning by such bodies will be fragmented, where the wheel is re-invented over and over again. A coordinated approach across interested parties is needed.

There is a barrier to effective cooperation, however. Because of the general complacency in Britain about child labour, there has been little informed debate and the complexities of the issues are not yet widely understood. One of the main functions of research such as has been discussed in this book is to encourage an awareness of the fact that child labour is not simply a problem in Britain but a problem to which there are no easy solutions. In our opinion the tendency for school pupils to take part-time work is not a pattern of behaviour which will just 'go away'. There is evidence that, as pupils move up through the school years, more of them are involved in work.

We saw in Chapter 4 that more pupils in Year 12 were working than had been working in Year 10. This trend is confirmed by more recent research we have undertaken which is as yet unpublished. School pupils in the later years of Scottish schools, 5th and 6th year, were more likely to be working than those in earlier years. Not only were more students working in these later years, but they were committing longer hours to work. All of this while they were preparing for examinations which could have a major influence on their future careers.

There is evidence that it is increasingly common to find students in higher education combining study with work (Callender and Kempson, 1996). This development has been linked to changing funding patterns. Changing government policies on higher education make it unlikely that there will ever again be large enough grants to fully cover student subsistence. If this is so, the pattern of higher levels of part-time employment among students is likely to continue. If this comes to be regarded as the norm, it seems likely to have an effect on pupils in the later stages of secondary education. There is already quite a strong trend for these pupils to work. If they see their forthcoming years at college or university as being a time of part-time employment too, this must surely increase the likelihood that senior school pupils will regard having a job as simply foreshadowing the life style they can expect in their coming years. Has an equivalent of Dearing enquiry been initiated to looking to finances of secondary school students?

The second conclusion to emerge from the research is that we have tended in the recent past to idealize children's work in Britain. The prevailing image, and once again government ministers have helped to create this illusion, is of children delivering newspapers for 'pocket money'. The European Union has been portrayed as threatening newspaper delivery, although any one taking the trouble to read the documents would discover this was not the case. Research evidence requires us not to give up the notion of the 'paper-boy' or 'paper-girl', since such jobs do exist, but we must broaden our notion of the jobs that children actually undertake. The more we are aware of the wide variety of jobs children do, the more we are likely to have to question whether all such work should be protected. We may be happy that children serve in a shop on a Saturday, or wait at table. But what if the shop is a fast-food take-away, such as the traditional fish and chip shop, and the child has to work with hot fat? And what if, rather than serve at a restaurant table, the child is working in the kitchen. We may then look at the details of work, in a garage, say, or on a building site, and conclude that opportunity to acquire skills in these environments is balanced by considerable dangers to health and safety.

If we allow ourselves to be critical and analytical about children's jobs, then we need to look again at the 'traditional' jobs. Newspaper delivery takes place in winter as well as summer, in the dark as well as the light. Newspapers can be heavy. 'Delivery' is not always a complete description of the job; sometimes the paper-boy or paper-girl is expected to collect payment from customers, putting them at risk of attack. When delivery is undertaken by bicycle, the possibility of road accidents arises.

In the United States, Mortimer et al. (1994) argue that there is evidence of a 'career path' in child employment. Younger children started employment in the delivery sector and 'graduated' to shop work as they moved through the school years. For Mortimer and his colleagues, the types of jobs carried out by the older students had a greater potential for offering the individual some form of skill acquisition. The results in Cumbria and in our recent unpublished research in Scotland tend to suggest a similar trend in Britain, as far as the jobs undertaken are concerned. However, we would warn against taking too optimistic a view on such trends. We would require much closer analysis of the actual jobs before being able to conclude that the opportunity for training and skill acquisition improved as students moved to different jobs in the later years.

What these results do is to suggest that child employment is firmly rooted in the economy. This economic participation is generally overlooked and has not been evaluated, either in terms of the contribution made by this form of employment nor the implications if it were removed. Periodic surveys are undertaken to examine the role of children as consumers. However, the source of their spending power tends to be ignored as an issue. Similarly, their role as participants in the economy is not given the attention it deserves. The relative cheapness and low status of this form of employee make them the ultimate flexible labour force. Lavalette (1996) is clearly of this view, arguing that by its very nature the relationship is exploitative.

Investigation of the type of work carried out by British children may lead us to conclude that whatever problems exist for children in Britain they are trivial compared with those facing children in Latin America, Asia, Africa and Eastern Europe. These differences will partly reflect the nature of the culture and the economy in which children live. However, while the jobs are qualitatively different, one might argue that there are underlying similarities between children in situations which are superficially very different. The fundamental nature of the relationship between employer and employee is the same. In both cases, children have little or no bargaining power in the relationship.

The third issue that emerges from the research findings is that the current means of controlling child employment in Britain is clearly not effective. Whichever aspect of the law concerning the employment of children one considers, one finds a substantial gap between what Parliament prescribed and what actually takes place. Children begin working before they have reached the age of 13; they start their work before seven o'clock in the morning; they continue work after seven o'clock in the evening; they work in kitchens, bars and factories; they work without permits from the local authorities; and so on. In every instance the legislation is failing. In 1996 the Department of Health circulated a consultative document in which it proposed harmonization of bylaws governing child employment between local authorities and some modest changes in when children may work and what jobs they may do. The two most striking features of this document were, first, its failure to take account of the fact that existing bylaws are widely ignored and, second, its failure to address questions of implementation.

That the legislation is not applied means that the possibility of exploiting those it is intended to protect is more likely. In Appendix 2, we give a sample of largely self-explanatory newspaper headlines which indicate that exploitation does indeed take place. In some cases, of course, these headlines refer to court cases in which the law is being applied. However, we must stress that sometimes the law acts too late to avoid abuse and with too little force to act as a deterrent.

The final issue which we must address is the 'commonsense' notion that children's part-time work is of itself a 'good thing'. This notion is based upon the rather simplistic analysis that children are moving towards adulthood and that part-time employment introduces them to adult roles and the world of work. Yes, it can be the case that having a part-time job can be a positive experience. It is naive, however, to assume that this will be the norm, without adequate evaluation of what it is that could make the experience potentially rewarding.

British evidence on what is potentially beneficial and potentially harmful in children's jobs is scarce. There is enough American evidence, however, to make us confident that broad generalizations about 'children's jobs' are unhelpful. We must differentiate between types of jobs, the hours worked, when these hours are worked, what exactly the job entails, and so on. All need to be closely scrutinized. It is important to note that we are not arguing that researchers will be able to say that if a child is employed in job 'X' for 'Y' number of hours per week that the outcome will be positive. As in adult employment, there are no guarantees in this area. What we are arguing is that the issue requires serious study and monitoring. Only with an adequate research base will we be able to minimize the negative aspects of this experience.

While the material in this book may allow us to challenge the level of complacency that surrounds this issue in Britain, it fails to answer a different question. What causes child employment? The present material may not answer this question but it does shed some light on the feasibility of some suggested explanations.

In an earlier study (Lavalette et al., 1991) we drew attention to two popular explanations. First, there is the poverty explanation, where it is argued that children are driven to work because of family poverty. Second, the reserve army hypothesis, which is that children are drawn into the labour market due to the lack of available adult employees. (See Lavalette, 1994, for a more detailed discussion of these models.)

It was not an aim of the research we have been reporting to provide evidence on the causes of child employment. However, some of our findings do have some bearing on the standing of these theories. In particular, we have shown first, in North Tyneside, that children in a school in a relatively deprived area had a similar level of work experience to children in a relatively more affluent area, and, second, in Blackburn in a relatively deprived area we found somewhat lower levels of work than in other parts of the country. The poverty hypothesis would lead us to expect a higher number of employed children in those schools with the highest levels of poverty. That this was not the case suggests that poverty is not the sole 'cause' of child employment.

The second hypothesis relates levels of child employment to lack of available adult workers. If this were the case we would expect to see some regional variation in employment levels reflecting differing levels of adult employment. Lavalette (1994) contrasted levels of child employment in areas with markedly different unemployment rates and found little evidence to show that children were more likely to be working where adult unemployment levels were low.

The present data shows a fairly consistent pattern of employment across all the studies carried out by us in a number of different regions. The studies by other researchers reviewed in Chapter 2 reinforces this view. Some variation does exist, for example in Cumbria. The students at the school in the Lake District showed the highest level of employment in the region. This may indicate that local employment variation may play a role in the level of child employment. However, the base level of employment appears to be embedded in society, showing little variation across the country. We have not been able to find any clear differences between rural and urban areas, but since the only rural data we have collected has been from the adjacent areas of Cumbria and Dumfries and Galloway, we do not rule out the possibility of differences emerging from studies covering wider areas of the country.

Explanations such as the poverty hypothesis and the reserve army hypothesis have been labelled as 'mono-causal' by Lavalette (1994). It is his position that explanations of this kind will founder simply because they fail to acknowledge the complex interaction between a range of factors. For Lavalette, child employment is ultimately rooted in the form of economy, a capitalist economy driven by profit motive simply means that children can be exploited to increase profit.

We suggested in Chapter 6 that Bronfenbrenner's ecological development model might help us understand the relationship between the child or adolescent's job and the wider social framework in which the job exists. It could be argued that a parallel exists between Bronfenbrenner's widest context, the 'macro-system', and Lavalette's argument that the nature of economic relationships is at the heart of any comprehension of child employment.

At present the causes of child employment in Britain and countries with similar economies is poorly understood, in part from lack of research. In underdeveloped countries a number of 'causes' have been identified. These include the lack of a universal comprehensive education system and the needs of growing economies in which striving for increased standards of living co-exist with labour-intensive production methods. Lavalette (1994) points out a number of researchers have borrowed this framework to analyse child employment in the developed West (for example, MacLennan et al., 1985; Fyfe, 1989). Let us reverse this trend and consider what child employment in the global 'North' might tell us about child employment in the 'South'.

Britain and the United States have compulsory education systems, are economically developed in terms of the levels and means of production, and have lower levels of relative poverty. Even in such circumstances children are working. What lessons are to be learnt from this? Is child employment 'inevitable'?

Perhaps the lesson to be taken from the Western economies is that economic development, compulsory education and reduced levels of poverty are not the solution to eliminating children's economic participation. What may happen is that the forms of child employment may change, but they will continue to be involved in the labour market. To many such a transition would, in and of itself, be deemed a success, if it were possible to remove many of the least acceptable types of jobs that are done by children. However, replacing certain forms of work with other types of jobs does not change the nature of the relationship between employee and employer.

The problem of tackling child employment throughout the world is a complex one and we do not mean to belittle the issue by oversimplifying the argument. However, it is necessary for the developed countries to realize that they have an issue of child employment in their own backyard. We, in Western Europe and the United States, should be cautious about adopting 'moral' positions about the exploitation of children in other countries and continents, while ignoring problems at home.

IMPLICATIONS

All of the evidence argues against the 'commonsense' notions that Britain does not have an issue to deal with in respect to child employment. If that is the case how do we tackle the problem within the British context?

A range of views have emerged which may be found in the limited debates surrounding this subject. At one extreme we have Roger Scruton (1990) arguing that children should be allowed to escape compulsory schooling for the world of work. In contrast we find Emma Nicholson expressing the view that children should be focusing on education not employment. At the time Nicholson was a Conservative MP and was attending a meeting of the House of Commons Employment Committee in May of 1991. In questioning the evidence provided by the Low Pay Unit, and, in particular, her response to the Low Pay Unit's position that children will always work, she raises doubts about their argument. Nicholson suggested that if work led to the development of a sense of responsibility then this could be attained in a number of alternative ways, for example in school, learning new sports. As for the income earned it was in her view so low that it was not a justification for working (House of Commons Employment Committee, 1991).

In between these views we find a form of compromise position. The Low Pay Unit argues that children will work and that this needs to accepted. From that position the way to ensure adequate protection is to have effective legislation. Ann Clwyd, the Labour MP, adopts this view in suggesting that children should be allowed to work but that it must be within a properly regulated framework.

In the political arena Scruton's position is unlikely to be followed. It would raise protests that we were returning to the worst excesses of Victorian Britain, that we would be failing children in terms of the principles of the education system. It is worth noting that Gillian Shepherd, the then Education Secretary, did comment that school children should be encouraged into work schemes (Carvel, 1995).

Emma Nicholson's position also seems problematic. In effect it would mean banning child employment and we think this raises some fundamental issues which we will return to later. For the moment we wish to focus on the pragmatic position taken by Ann Clwyd and the Low Pay Unit. Effective legislation would still allow children to work.

LEGISLATION

As already noted, the Department of Health recently proposed some changes in the regulation of child employment. One notable feature of the Department's proposed model bylaws for local authorities is that, unlike the bylaws previously produced as a results of the 1933 Act, it lists a set of acceptable forms of employment for children. Previously the system was to list prohibited jobs. Second, it has extended the days on which children can work to include Sunday, although the total number of hours which can be worked remains the same. Third, it maintains the permit system as the recommended way of monitoring children's work, although it clearly states that it should be the employer's responsibility to ensure that the school-aged worker has such a permit.

The consultation document needs to be viewed within its political context. The government of the day had arranged for a temporary opt-out of the European Union directive on child employment, arguing that current British legislation was adequate to the task. The consultation process undertaken by the Department of Health was presented as being a preparation for harmonization with other European Union countries once the opt-out comes to an end. In the circumstances, it is striking that the document proposes so few changes. One wonders why it was necessary to opt out on this issue, if so little needs to be done to meet the European standards.

At the time of writing this consultation document is in a form of limbo. The 1997 General Election has produced a change in government and a stated change in policy towards Europe. We will have to await the impact such a change may have on the specific issue of child employment.

Irrespective of which government is in office there is an obvious problem. Legislation has existed for many years, yet study after study indicates that it is ineffective. What evidence is there that any new legislation will be any more effective? For legislation to work it needs to be implemented and that requires a recognition that laws do not simply enforce themselves.

We would argue that if legislation is to be effective in monitoring child employment then it needs to meet the following criteria.

1. Formulation

It needs to be correctly formulated. By this we mean that the ideas embedded within the legislation must reflect our best knowledge on the topic. As they stand, the 1933 and 1937 Acts and the consultation document do not meet this criteria. There are three reasons why we would argue this.

First, the legislation allows children during term time to work up to 17 hours per week. On what basis was that figure chosen? In the American literature, the watershed lies between 15 and 20 hours per week. The limited British research suggests that the watershed may be lower, 10 hours per week. If the aim of the legislation is to allow children to be employed because of its potential benefits to them, then it could be argued that these can be achieved from working a small number of hours (as argued by Greenberger, 1983).

Second, the legislation relies upon the work permit system. At present, very few children have a permit. The consultation document suggests that employers become responsible for ensuring that permits are obtained and that begins to clear up some of the confusion as to whose responsibility this is. However, we believe that this system needs some more thought.

At present children require a new permit when they change jobs. We also know that children often move in and out of different jobs. This means that for every new job a different permit is required. The potential for bureaucratic drift is immense.

The permit system requires the involvement of school, the parents, the employers and the local authorities in order to process it. They each have a role to play before a permit can be issued. Given the number of children working and the amount of movement between jobs, it seems to us that local authorities would have to commit significant resources to keep up with this particular paper chase. Given such problems, some review of what the permit system is actually trying to do needs to be undertaken. If its aim is to monitor and ensure that children are working in acceptable conditions then alternative systems which are less problematic may be possible. For example, if a child wishes to work, then he or she could be issued with a permit which covers a range of employments, thus eliminating the need to re-apply every time a job is changed. The permit could include tear-off forms which the child could use to inform the relevant body of any change in their employment. An alternative system where employers are licensed allowing them to employ children could also be envisaged.

Third, the consultation document proposes the use of a prescribed list of acceptable jobs. It is argued that in indicating what is acceptable it will direct those who want to work into these specific types of jobs. The obvious question to arise is what is 'acceptable'? We would suggest that a consensus will arrive at a list of jobs which is derived from notions of social acceptability, historical precedence and 'commonsense'. There has been no objective study of what constitutes a sound basis for acceptability. This requires some clear discussion of what it is that we think children gain from work. Whether a form of employment is acceptable will depend on its ability to meet these criteria. To date no such discussion has taken place and no effective research on the impact of job type on outcomes exists.

2. Implementation

Can it be implemented? Responsibility for enforcement currently lies with local authorities. A number of possible reasons could be postulated to explain why most of them currently fall far short of meeting their responsibilities.

The first possible explanation is that local authorities, like the rest of society, did not perceive the issue as significant. The 'invisible' nature of the problem meant that the question of child employment did not make it on to their agenda.

During the middle years of the 1990s the subject has now achieved a higher profile.

In response to this a number of local authorities have moved the topic up their agendas and have taken some action to tackle issues raised by it. These initiatives have included local authorities commissioning research to establish the extent of the problem. Some authorities have appointed child employment officers to address the issue within their area, e.g. North Tyneside and Greenwich. In addition educational welfare officers in England, who usually have the responsibility of enforcing this legislation, have developed a 'network' through which they exchange ideas and information on child employment.

However, it must be acknowledged that while all these initiatives are welcome, the greatest constraint on local authorities effectively implementing this legislation is related to resources. Central government has argued that resources are already allocated to local authorities to monitor child employment and that the proposals within the Department of Health consultation document will have a 'zero sum effect', i.e. no extra costs are involved.

For the legislation to be implemented effectively the resource cost must be recognized. This requires local authorities to allocate an appropriate part of their budget to this issue and for central government to acknowledge that the scale of the phenomenon goes beyond original budgeting estimates.

3. Publicity

For legislation to be effective then it must be known about, particularly by those to whom it will apply and to whom it must seem credible. A number of different groups need to be aware of this legislation: employers, the schools, parents, children and the local authorities.

There is a limited amount of evidence regarding existing levels of awareness, unless we take non-compliance with the legislation as an indicator. If we assume that individuals would conform with the legislation if they knew about it, then the evidence would suggest that the majority do not know about it. A good deal of anecdotal information indicates that ignorance of this legislation is the norm.

One study of newsagents by a local authority showed that many of them were unaware of their responsibilities in this area (Renfrew District Environmental Services Department, 1995). A recent newspaper article testifies to the fact that many local authorities are unaware of their role as well (Sinclair, 1996)

Some local authorities have been trying to raise awareness of this issue. This is achieved by targeting schools and employers with information. We saw in Chapter 3 that one school in Dumfries and Galloway had a much higher level of permits compared to others because it had a pro-active approach to this topic. Classes on social education contained material on employment and the questions of legislation and permits were discussed. This suggests that positive and relatively inexpensive steps could be taken to improve levels of awareness among children and to improve levels of compliance with the legislation. However, the school involved in this study was in a rural community and it is possible that the local norms amongst employers played a part in making work permits more common.

Recently in a small pilot study we compared the effect of different levels of educational intervention on children's knowledge about child employment and their uptake of permits (Hobbs et al., 1996b, unpublished report). The results showed that there was a relationship between the level of intervention and children's awareness of child employment issues and legislative detail. The most intensive form of intervention involving class lessons based around video and workshop material had the greatest impact on knowledge levels. The results provide some grounds for optimism. However, we were singularly unsuccessful in raising the level of work permits held. In that sense we were able to show that a gap existed between children's knowledge and their behaviour.

Why should there be a failure to put knowledge into practice? A number of explanations are possible:

1. This is simply one aspect of a generally acknowledged feature of adolescent behaviour in our society. There is evidence that there are many areas where adolescents have knowledge which they fail to put into practice, e.g. risks of drugs, use of contraception.
2. It is possible that by informing children about the law they realize that they are working illegally and opt not to tell anyone since they believe it is unlikely that they would ever be found out.
3. Although knowing that a work permit may be obtained, when confronted with a bureaucratic system, the young worker decides that it is too much trouble to follow through.
4. Children may see the permit system as lacking relevance, since in their eyes there are no obvious benefits from holding a permit.

What is needed is an evaluation programme of intervention strategies where their effectiveness is measured against specific criteria. In addition it has to be accepted that education is not targeted only at the potential employees, it also needs to be directed at parents, teachers and employers.

If effective legislation is to be used in tackling the question of child employment we clearly have a long way to go, with policy makers having to address a number of fundamental problems.

An alternative legislative strategy would be to prohibit child employment. This position shares some of the problems noted in adopting controlling legislation. It would still require resources, commitment to implement it, and awareness of the legislation. There may also be some problem in defining what is actually prohibited.

To proceed down the prohibition route one would need to justify the loss of potential benefits which may be obtained within a properly regulated framework. One possible argument would be to demonstrate that the benefits associated with part-time employment could be attained from other sources, for example within the school system or within some school-based work experience programme. At present we are unable to resolve this issue due to the lack of research in this area.

There is another issue that those who wish to prohibit child employment have to address. In effect it resorts to a paternalistic stance that adults know best when it comes to decisions relating to children. This is hardly consistent with United Nations Convention on the Rights of the Child. Article 12 argues that children's voices should be listened to and that they should have an input into decisions affecting them. This does not mean that the child's view dominates, rather it implies that dialogue and joint decision-making guarantees the right of all parties to be heard. To the best of our knowledge those in favour of prohibiting child employment have not asked children what their views are. It is also worth noting the recent consultation document on revising legislation did not canvass the opinion of those that it would directly affect, the children.

There is some evidence that children may in fact be opposed to attempts to prohibit them from working. Murray (1991) found that the majority of children in her study wanted the right to work. That is not the same as saying they wished to be exploited. A similar conclusion emerged from focus group discussions carried out by the present authors. In this case the participants believed part-time employment to be acceptable while at school and they highlighted the benefits they perceived. They also indicate that much of this work is carried out for instrumental reasons, or as a way of combatting boredom (Hobbs et al., 1996b, unpublished report). We will return to this data later. For the moment it allows us to raise the point that those who experience employment have legitimate views and yet have no forum through which they can be heard. Lavalette argues that this is an example of the 'age hierarchy', a 'socially constructed phenomenon' (Lavalette, 1996: 179). The effect of this is that those in junior positions in the hierarchy cannot achieve full social status.

If we accept the legitimacy of the UN Convention then children's views must be incorporated into this debate. Accepting children's views may rule out the prohibition of child employment but it would not preclude legislating to limit exploitation.

Lavalette (1996) questions the efficacy of the legislative route. For Lavalette the 'solution' to child employment is to be found in changing 'capitalist social relations'. While acknowledging the difficulty in achieving this, Lavalette questions whether legislation will be effective in our current form of economy.

Lavalette is sceptical about the validity of relying on commonsense in formulating legislation and making decisions on this subject. One challenge which researchers face is in devising means by which the distinction between 'good' and 'bad' forms of employment can be identified. Failure to tackle this issue, however problematic, will simply leave the discussion dominated by the uninformed 'commonsense' school of policy making.

RESEARCH ISSUES

When we look at the research on child employment in Britain we are faced with a number of obvious gaps in our understanding. These gaps fall into two distinct categories. First, there is a severe limitation on how much we know about the nature and extent of work by children and adolescents of school age. Second, research has only begun to look at the role of influential variables.

1. Nature and Extent

In this book we have presented a review of current research in Britain. This work has been largely devoted to attempts to establish how many children are working and what they are doing. This bias was partly driven by the lack of central government figures. We would argue that the 'nature and extent' debate is largely resolved. The fact that when government-sponsored research was eventually undertaken (Hibbett and Beatson, 1995), the findings were quite compatible with those of previous independent researchers, including the present authors, means that the broad picture of child labour is now clear. Attention must now begin to focus on more detailed, specific questions.

A start has been made in trying to understand the gender differences which seem to exist in children's work. Other important distinctions have barely been touched upon. We have found no clear evidence of class differences in the extent of employment undertaken, but further studies might show important differences in types of jobs, attitudes to work and ways of spending earned income between different social classes. We have already pointed out how limited our investigations into differences between urban and rural area have been. The very notion of 'urban versus rural' may well turn out to be too crude. Ethnicity is also urgently in need of research, in part because, as with so many aspects of child labour, a number of stereotypes can be found which are not supported by any evidence. Child members of some ethnic communities are often pictured as working long hours unpaid in family businesses such as corner shops.

Most studies of child labour in Britain have not attended to issues of ethnicity partly because many of the sample populations did not reflect a significant ethnic mix. However, there are a few exceptions. Jolliffe et al.'s (1995) study was based in Greenwich and included an ethnically diverse population, although it must be noted that some of the ethnic groups were represented by small numbers. In this study 41 per cent of the total sample were found to be working and this is taken as a base line when looking at group variations. When considering ethnic group variations, 42 per cent of English/Scottish/Welsh pupils were working; 33 per cent of Indian; 44 per cent of Caribbean; 45 per cent of mixed and 45 per cent of other. The question of sample size is brought home when we look at the Caribbean group, while 44 per cent were working this was from a total sample of 59 children who classified themselves in this way from an overall sample of 1,600 children.

Jolliffe et al. interpret their findings as showing that Indian, Pakistani and Bangladeshi groups were less likely to be working. They argue that this contradicts the stereotype of children from such ethnic groups working in family businesses. This interpretation is slightly problematic. Although Jolliffe et al. do include family employment in their definition of work they do not look at ethnic breakdown according to job type. For example, it may be that fewer children in these ethnic groups are working but those that are may be employed in specific types of jobs.

That this interpretation is possible receives some support from Pond and Searle's (1991) study, which centred on Birmingham and included a wide range of ethnic groups. Of the total sample, 23 per cent were Asian, 10 per cent Afro-Caribbean and 3 per cent other.

They argue that their results show that Asian children are less likely to work. This argument is based upon comparison of proportions and no statistical analysis is used to assess if these variations are significant. In addition they argue that Asian children, contrary to stereotypes, are not involved in family businesses. Once again we see some confusion in the presentation of their data. Pond and Searle's results show that while fewer Asian children were working the majority of those who were working, 61 per cent, were involved in family businesses. This is compared with 31 per cent of white/European and 8 per cent of Afro-Caribbean children employed in family businesses.

In the study carried out in Blackburn we found that black and Asian children were less likely to be involved in paid employment outside of the family (Lavalette et al., 1996). Nor did we find any evidence that large numbers of Asian children were working for their families. This does not rule out the possibility that those that do work find employment in specific types of jobs.

All of these studies indicate a lower level of employment among minority ethnic groups. However, the studies to date have tended to confuse the numbers employed with the forms of employment. This lack of clarity simply highlights the fact that further research is needed. It must be noted that in carrying out this research a number of methodological problems will have to be addressed. It will be necessary to consider the definition of employment used in such studies. Clear operational definitions of the different forms of employment will be needed if a better understanding is to emerge. It may also be the case that the traditional form of data-collecting, questionnaire, may not be the best way to proceed.

Throughout our research we have defined employment as paid employment outside of the family. In adopting this definition we were consciously acknowledging that children's economic participation can take many forms. The most obvious is working within the family, in either a paid or unpaid capacity. In addition, studies of children's contribution to household duties warrants consideration as well (see Goodnow, 1988).

The different forms of employment require separate study but will pose researchers with a number of problems. The difficulty in studying children's work within the household was highlighted in the study undertaken in Blackburn. The major difficulty was in the form of data collecting. Like other studies of child employment, this study used a questionnaire designed to collect information. In designing this questionnaire we had to confront the difficulties in differentiating between the subtleties of the various forms of economic activity. We will return to this subject later.

2. Influencing Variables

In Chapter 5 we noted the extent to which research into the relationship between hours worked and academic performance showed that this relationship is not linear. Such studies need to be extended and their replicability checked. Once a more substantial body of evidence has been accumulated, we might be better able to offer an objective evaluation of the point at which legislation should set about controlling the number of hours children are allowed to work.

This preliminary work needs to be extended to include job type and its influence on maximizing the potential benefits to be gained from this experience. However, in targeting variables in this way we need to keep in mind the concerns of writers such as Mortimer and Finch (1996). They argue that research needs to attend to the wider context within which employment takes place. It is only within this framework that a better understanding of the impact of child employment will be gained.

In Britain this issue of 'wider context' has not been addressed. For example there are no studies which consider the relationship of parental attitude or family context to child employment. How do parents view their children's experience? Do they exert control over the income earned? Do they encourage or discourage it? It is only in addressing these questions that we will gain some insight into the influence that the context exerts on the interpretation of attitudes towards work, education and the work ethic.

METHODOLOGICAL ISSUES

We have already noted that data collecting in this field has been dominated by the questionnaire. In many cases we have come across examples where questions on part-time employment are incorporated within a wider ranging survey. Balding's work and the recent Trades Union Congress survey are two examples of this style. Of necessity such an approach means that a limited number of questions are posed and some of the subtleties of children's part-time work is lost.

There are a number of studies which, using questionnaires, have focused solely on employment, for example Pond and Searle (1991) and our own work. These studies do allow for a more detailed consideration of the work experience but even here there are still limitations. One issue is the accuracy of recall, particularly on retrospective questions such as the age of first employment.

Researchers need to be vigilant in monitoring the reliability of their findings. An example of how this may be done can be seen in our own studies. Most of our work has collected information from 14- to 16-year-old school pupils. One of the questions requires them to indicate age of first paid employment outside of the family. We regularly got reports that children had worked before 13 years of age, the legal minimum age. One study allowed us to check the reliability of this claim. In this case the sample was the whole secondary school below the school-leaving age. A high degree of consistency emerged in terms of the levels of employment claimed in their retrospective data and the numbers recorded as current workers in the lower school years (Lavalette et al., 1995).

With proper monitoring, the claims made by questionnaire data can be shown to be reliable. However, there are limitations to the type of information that can be collected in this way. Our Blackburn study provided valuable information on work within and outwith the family but it also drew attention to the difficulty of collecting this type of information in this way. While the researchers may feel that their questions are clear and concise it is important to remember the target group who will have to interpret these questions and answer them. Pupils in the early years of secondary school do not necessarily have very highly developed reading and comprehension skills.

The targeting of the relevant population can also provide a number of challenges for researchers. Our studies have focused on pupils within the school system, a form of captive sample. This makes sense given that we are looking at those children under 16 years of age, still within the compulsory education framework. Our strategy, which has focused upon those children in the 14–16-year-old age group, has been to include the whole of the relevant school population, i.e. no subsampling was used. The return rates on all of our studies have been high but not perfect. Absentees were followed up, but in each case a number of pupils on the school role were unfortunately excluded from the survey. This group may be absent for a range of reasons, including work commitments. Two issues need to be addressed. First, does the omission of these pupils result in an underestimation of the numbers involved in employment, and, second, does the group omitted from the study differ in any significant way from those pupils who work but were attending school? Further investigation of such absentee groups is warranted. Absentees may include children who have dropped out of the school system entirely. Such individuals are clearly harder to study than those regularly attending school, but the possibility that the work problems they face may be of a much more serious order makes it important that they be studied. There is a growing body of evidence of the widespread existence of child prostitution in Britain (see, for example, Jesson, 1993; Lee and O'Brien, 1995). This cannot be ignored when trying to develop an accurate account of the working lives of British children.

As we saw in Chapter 2, some studies fail to provide an adequate breakdown of employment related to the different age groups, e.g. Pond and Searle (1991).

Since those studies which do distinguish between children on the basis of age show clear age differences, we hope that all future research will either confine itself to fixed and identified age groups or treat age as a potentially significant variable. In a recent study comparing the work habits of school pupils above and below the minimum school-leaving age, we found evidence of a change in the amount of time committed to work and the types of work undertaken (McKechnie et al., unpublished). Such findings reinforce the need to differentiate between children of different ages.

Another aspect of work which some researchers fail to take into account is what might be termed the dynamic nature of child employment. The distinction we have made between 'current' and 'former' workers is an attempt to do at least some justice to this factor. Questions such as 'Do you have a job?' or 'Have you had a job in the past year?' may give misleading impressions, if the reality is that some children move in and out of jobs during the years of secondary education. The questions we asked were a poor substitute for a much better sort of investigation, namely longitudinal studies. These alone will be able to give a completely adequate picture of movements in and out of jobs. Of course, there is also the question of why children leave jobs, and why they return to work, not to mention why some children never work at all.

The data we presented in Chapter 4 of a relatively limited (and initially unplanned) longitudinal study in Cumbria only hints at what a more fully and carefully planned look at children's work over several years might be able to tell us.

There is an additional reason for employing longitudinal designs, namely, the question of causality. The limited British research that has addressed the implications of child employment suggests a link between work and education. At present these studies have not been able to identify the direction of causality. American studies have shed some light on this debate and indicate two processes at work (Steinberg et al., 1993). First, excessive commitment to work has a negative effect on education. Second, poor educational performance can result in a higher commitment to work. Not only are both processes at work but they will also interact with each other. It is necessary to see if such findings emerge within the British context.

Irrespective of the findings it could be argued that from an educational perspective both processes give cause for alarm. In the first case, outside commitment to part-time work may limit educational achievement. Short-term financial gain replaces longer term benefits that accrue from higher educational attainment. The second scenario suggests that students failing or underperforming at school may choose to opt out to devote more energies to part-time work. In doing so they may simply compound their problems.

The two scenarios raise questions for the education system. How do they encourage students to adopt a long-term perspective when viewing their education.

The second issue relates to how schools deal with students who are not performing well in academic terms. If a more vocational orientation is thought to be of benefit to this group, should it be left to the individual child to gain this experience within the 'free labour market' without support?

Unfortunately we have no specific solution to suggest, other than this issue needs to be considered as part of the educational debate regarding the balance between vocational and academic orientations within the school system.

Tackling the question of causality has obvious implications for research design. However, at a more fundamental level, researchers may need to be open to the development of alternative methodologies. If we take seriously the United Nations Convention on the Rights of the Child, we need to move towards research techniques that allow us to capture the specific voices of children. Listening to children's views and perspectives is not part of a move towards 'child power'. Rather it is a means of extending participation. Such approaches may also start to address some of Lavalette's (1996) concerns about the 'age hierarchy' and the extent to which this affects who is listened to.

Researchers in underdeveloped countries have been at the forefront of developing such strategies. A number of non-governmental organizations have used such approaches in developing strategies to tackle child employment issues. For example, ActionAid demonstrates the way that the children's point of view can be gained by adopting a range of techniques where the emphasis was on participation. These included interviews, discussion groups, task-ranking exercises, mobility maps drawn by the children themselves (see Johnson et al., 1995). Such an approach moves us away from the closed questionnaire design that has dominated research in Britain to embrace more open-ended forms of data-collecting.

Recently the International Working Group on Child Labour (IWGCL) has adopted as a central tenet of its programme the belief that children's voices will provide a degree of insight into working children that has so far been lacking. This approach has led to the development of a child-centred strategy where working children are brought together to express their views and to provide suggestions for tackling the problems that working children face. In a recent example of this approach, working children from Asia, Africa and Latin America were brought together to create a forum for their voices to be heard, the International Movement of Working Children.

In a short video released by the IWGCL, entitled *Time To Listen*, children from different geographical regions display an awareness of shared experience and discuss their position in a way which shows a degree of insight which many adults may find surprising. The participants put forward the view that elimination of child employment is unlikely and that strategies need to be pragmatic. For example, they advocated structuring school systems so that working children can be accommodated rather than excluded. What emerges is a view that, for this particular group, what is important is that they are recognized as having rights, including the right to work, and that their status should not be used to discriminate between themselves and other workers.

One of the potential problems in adopting these techniques is that they move researchers towards more qualitative forms of data. The tensions between quantitative and qualitative forms of data-collecting have resulted in an ongoing debate regarding their respective benefits and problems. More recently texts have started to appear addressing the practicalities of using some of these methods in research (Vaughn et al., 1996). Rather than viewing this form of data as competing with more traditional ideas which stress quantifiable data, the challenge is one of how to integrate these approaches. In doing so we are more likely to gain a greater degree of insight into specific issues such as child employment.

Among British research such approaches have rarely been used. Mizen (1992) has been an exception in that he used interviews as part of his data-collecting process. The present authors have also used semi-structured interviews and focus group techniques. One study, using one-to-one interviews, was designed to cast some light onto Green's (1990) claim that part-time employment should be viewed more positively. In particular Green argued that we need to acknowledge the degree of control that children exert over their work experience. The results from these interviews indicated that the main form of control was one of withdrawing one's labour, in other words quitting the job. (We have come across little evidence of children in contemporary Britain withdrawing their labour by striking.) The interview material suggests that the nature of the job experience was one where they had no control over their environment or participation in work. Despite this, the majority of those interviewed argued that their part-time work experience was of long-term benefit to them. One interviewee supported this by claiming that his part-time job was of value because a record of employment would be of value '…to show that I can work' (McKechnie et al., 1996).

In another attempt to gain some insight into children's views on their work, focus group techniques were employed. Rather than one-to-one interviews, small groups of school students were brought together with a 'facilitator' present. The role of the facilitator was to encourage discussion of a range of topics related to employment and to follow up on spontaneous issues raised by the group when in discussion with each other.

The aim of the study was to explore a number of themes that had emerged from the one-to-one interviews. This would, on the one hand, allow us to check whether we could generalize from our findings and, on the other, allow related issues to be raised. From the discussions, it emerged that children have views on their pay levels and the need for regulation of child employment, particularly relating to the establishment of their rights. In these groups the dominant view to emerge was that they should be allowed to work if they so desire. The participants in these groups highlighted what they saw as the benefits of gaining work experience. These included the opportunity to work alongside older people and providing them with experience of the work environment. Once again the majority thought their work would be of value in the future:

> Shows you are independent and that you can work for your money.

> Teaches you to work with people and accept other people's point of view.

One may not feel comfortable with some of the views which children express but it is evident that they have opinions on issues relating to their lives. That children are able to deal with complex issues relating to employment is clearly demonstrated in another attempt to listen to children's ideas. Morrow asked children between the ages of 11 and 16 years of age to write an essay on what they thought children's rights should be. It is worth noting that the concept of a 'right' was not explained. The main concern reflected in these essays were with being respected and trusted, they wanted to be treated 'as people'.

One 12-year-old expressed her views in the following way:

> Children shouldn't be treated as cheap, slave labour on markets or checkouts. We are decent hard-working employees just like anyone else ... I also think children should be treated more like adults and if we don't understand not treat us like babies. I think the world should be open to us. (Morrow, 1989)

A 15-year-old wrote:

> I think children's rights are important because we are people too and shouldn't be treated like low lifes just because we are younger. I think kids deserve the same sort of respect that we are expected to give to so-called adults ... One issue that annoys me is that we aren't allowed a part-time job until your're 15, sometimes 16. This is stupid because if you want to earn some extra money you should be allowed because if you are 13 or 15 you may be as capable and responsible as a 15- or 16-year-old working somewhere. (Morrow, 1989)

We are not arguing that such studies are not without their difficulties, but what they do show is that a number of techniques could be explored. These examples, though, go beyond this, indicating that children know that many of them work, it is a common experience yet they have no rights at work. Their solution is to allow them to work but provide adequate protection and fair reward.

Adopting such techniques is no doubt problematic, not least from a methodological point of view. However, one of the main problems will be with adults accepting the legitimacy of the voice of children particularly in societies dominated by an 'age hierarchy'. Such approaches can add a new perspective to our understanding of child employment and researchers should accept the challenge of trying to integrate such techniques into their specific academic disciplines.

We believe that there is also a need for a greater conceptual clarity in research on child labour. Since we began research into this subject, we have been uncomfortable with the distinction which some writers make between 'child labour' and 'child work'. It dichotomizes employment in an apparently simple way, the 'acceptable' (child work) and the 'not acceptable' (child labour) forms of children's economic participation. The fundamental problem is that no clear, systematic system has been devised that allows us to evaluate which category any specific form of employment falls into (see Lavalette et al., 1991; Lavalette, 1994).

In addition it misrepresents the position of work within the child's life. If we think about adult employment, we do not think about adult work and adult labour. Instead we recognize that any particular job may lie somewhere along a dimension of positive and negative. Acceptable and unacceptable forms of work are simply the extremes. Why should we not accept that children's employment also forms a dimension along which a number of positions are possible?

In the last few years a number of pressures have resulted in an alternative model emerging to facilitate our understanding of child employment. This partly stems from the momentum created by the International Working Group on Child Labour. It takes the form of a 'continuum' (Feinstein, 1997). It replaces the dichotomy of work–labour with an acceptance that work may be 'beneficial' or 'intolerable', but that a number of positions lie in between. This model assumes that in placing an individual child's experience on the continuum we need to consider other variables such as the age, gender, ability of the child and the form of occupation and the child's experience within it.

In her paper, Feinstein argued that contextual factors had to be considered as well. This produced the notion of a 'matrix'. She appeared to suggest that the micro- and macro-economic aspects of a culture would have to be considered alongside the continuum. It is worth noting that the presentation seemed to be assuming a specific set of contextual factors. For example, the matrix did not appear to acknowledge that many children in the developed countries combine work and education, or that the relationship between work and education is not necessarily uni-directional. However, it is possible to conceive of a bi-directional relationship. Such assumptions may limit the model's applicability to a range of cultural contexts where children work.

Our main concern, however, is the 'continuum'. In trying to think how researchers and practitioners would apply this model it seemed to us that a number of problems arose.

1. It is unclear how one defines the extremes of the continuum. What is 'beneficial' and what is 'intolerable'. Have we simply replaced one semantic argument about 'work-labour' with a new one about 'beneficial–intolerable'? The model needs to make clear how these extremes are defined.
2. The relationship between the variables identified as important (gender, age, ability, conditions of work and occupation) and the continuum is unclear. It appears that these variables may be serving two purposes. First,

these variables define where on the continuum someone lies. Second, they also seem to be the basis for defining the continuum itself (beneficial–intolerable and points in between).

This would create problems for researchers since the variables that are linked causally to the outcome are also used in the definition of the outcome. From a research perspective there appears to be no clear separation between the independent variables (i.e. 'causes') and the dependent variables (i.e. 'effects').

The notion of a continuum has many positive aspects in that it encourages us to re-conceptualize children's employment. In particular it encourages us to accept that work can in some circumstances be 'beneficial'. We suggest that if we are to advance our understanding of children's employment, we need to be able to understand what influences the balance between the good and bad aspects of work. This conceptualization of the issue draws on the American research of Greenberger and Steinberg (1986) and Mortimer and Finch (1996).

From a research perspective, we see a need to work towards clear operational definitions of what constitutes a cost or benefit of employment. When we have specified a potential cost or benefit, it becomes possible to examine under what circumstances, if any, costs and benefits emerge. The costs and benefits remain mere hypotheses until we have demonstrated particular relationships with work.

For example, if we believe that employment is beneficial to education then it should be possible to show the link between these two variables. We would need to define what is meant by educational success (a crude definition might be exam performance) and then look at those aspects of work (hours, job type, and so on) which might be related to the educational outcome.

If one adopts this approach an alternative way of looking at the issues begins to emerge, namely a 'balance' model. In Figure 7.1 are listed a few of the costs and benefits which some studies have linked to children's employment.

The questions for researchers then becomes what influences the balance between the costs and benefits of work. Alternatively, we might want to think about how we tip the balance so that the good or beneficial aspects of work dominate. As with adult employment, we will never eliminate 'costs' completely, but we look for ways in which they can be minimized.

Costs	Benefits
'Bad'	'Good'
Health and safety	Autonomy
Limits free time	Self-reliance
Negative effect on education	Economic/business knowledge
Instrumentalism	Work experience
Less parent/peer contact	

FIGURE 7.1 Examples of costs and benefits of child employment.

In attempting to establish what will influence the costs and benefits of work, a number of specific variables will need to be studied. These include the number of hours worked, the type of job being done, when the hours are worked, gender and age. It is also anticipated that these variables will interact with each other as well.

The advantage of this model is that all of the variables, those within the balance and the variables which may influence the balance, can be investigated, they can be operationalized and clearly defined. As researchers we may disagree with how someone else defines a variable but at least, if it is clearly defined, it would be clear what is meant by the term in question.

This model is also flexible in that it can acknowledge that the context will play a role in defining the balance itself. The 'continuum' model attempts to do this by referring to the 'matrix'. We have already raised some doubts about the assumptions underlying that concept.

Any model that aims to allow us to understand the impact of employment on children faces a major hurdle. That hurdle is that children work in a wide range of economic and cultural contexts. In our approach, it is acknowledged that the 'balance' does not exist in a vacuum. The context within which the balance debate is taking place needs to be considered. By context we are referring to the social, developmental and cultural factors.

For example, in Britain research has considered the part-time work of pre-16-year-olds. Within our culture adolescence is perceived as a transition between childhood and adulthood, work may facilitate or inhibit this transition. What is important is that in the debate about the balance between costs and benefits of work in this context such a view of development would play a role in defining the nature of the balance.

This would then lead us to the conclusion that there will be no universal list of variables that are in the balance equation. The cultural context will define them.

We are not suggesting that this model is without problems. For example, it does not deal with the problem of weighting the variables in the balance equation; are some of the costs or benefits more important than others? However, adopting this form of model does have some advantages. First, it requires practitioners and researchers to move away from semantic arguments about 'work–labour' and to investigate systematically the child's experience of work. Second, it emphasizes that 'solutions' to child employment will vary from culture to culture, no universal solutions will be found. Third, it provides a framework for evaluating child employment in a range of cultures, be they developed or underdeveloped countries.

It may be helpful for us to spell out what we consider the role of the researcher to be and how we see the researcher as relating to other people. In Figure 7.2, we outline the activities of the researcher.

It may appear that we have failed to give a place to the child's perspective in the model. However, the researcher is part of a three-way relationship with the child and the policy maker.

Input
Hypotheses, questions;
Concepts, assumptions;
Evidence.

Features studied
Context, e.g. economic-family structure;
Child, e.g. age, gender;
Work, e.g. hours, tasks, physical conditions;
Outcomes for child, e.g. health, educational achievement.

Outcome
Demonstrated relationships among features studied.

FIGURE 7.2 Role of the researcher.

In Figure 7.3, pathway A represents the fact that the views of the child are one sort of evidence influencing the researcher. The child may also have an opportunity to express his or her views directly to the policy maker. However, since the researcher also addresses the policy maker (pathway B), this is also, in effect, an indirect way in which the child's views may come to influence the policy maker.

A Researcher – Child
B Researcher – Policy maker
C Policy maker – Child

FIGURE 7.3 Two-way channels of influence.

By proposing such a role for researchers in this area the importance of developing an adequate model to aid our understanding of child employment becomes self-evident. The balance model proposed does not answer all of our questions but provides a platform from which to develop our knowledge of the impact of children's economic participation.

SUMMING-UP

In this final chapter we have tried to draw attention to the implications of the research in this area and to show where gaps exist in our understanding.

Consideration of the present level of knowledge leads us to argue that we need to reject the 'myths' of child employment that exist in Britain. Given that we have defined employment in a way which some might argue is too narrow, it may be that children's contribution to the economy may be even greater.

Policy makers and educationalists need to address this issue, targeting adequate research and resources at the issues. There is a need for a serious debate about the role of work and education for those still within the compulsory school system. This debate needs to incorporate the views of children. Adults need to accept that children have a right to be heard.

APPENDIX 1   A NOTE ON SOURCES

We have referenced published printed material in the normal way. However, it seems appropriate to note two additional types of sources which we have found helpful.

TELEVISION DOCUMENTARIES

Television is a powerful way in which people's conceptions of child labour are formed and we are happy to acknowledge the part it has played in increasing our awareness. Because of the nature of television as a medium, these programmes are not so easily accessible for future reference as are printed works. This applies particularly to items that are contributions to news or magazine programmes. Nevertheless, we think it appropriate to give an indication of some of the main documentaries on which we have drawn.

Child Slaves   International perspective. Produced and directed by Peter Lee-Wright. BBC Community Programme Unit, 1989.

Children of the Loom   Main focus: India. Producer: Simon Berthon. *World in Action* series, Granada Television, 1985.

Children in Chains   International perspective. Director: Hubert Dubois. *Dispatches* series, CAPA/M6 Production for Channel 4, 1994.

Look who's Working   Main focus: Britain. Produced and directed by Marc Sigworth. *Undercover Britain* series, Channel 4, 1994.

Painted Babies   Main focus: child beauty competitions in the USA. Produced and directed by Jane Treays. BBC Bristol, 1996.

Turning a Blind Eye   Main focus: Britain. Producer: Dippy Chaudhary. *Public Eye* series, BBC News and Current Affairs, 1991.

What Price the Born-to-spend Generation?   Main focus: Scotland. Producer: Elizabeth Scobie. *Scottish Reporters* series, Redlight Production for Scottish Television, 1994.

INTERNATIONAL WORKING GROUP ON CHILD LABOUR (IWGCL)

We have been associated with the IWGCL since 1995. At the time of writing, its reports on particular countries, on regions, and on the world-wide circumstances of child workers have not yet been published. However, we had access to much IWGCL material, including draft reports and we believe our understanding of child labour has been thereby enhanced.

Our contributions to the IWGCL fall into three categories. We have edited two national reports, those on Great Britain and on the United States of America. We have also been responsible for drafting the regional report covering Europe. In this last case, we have drawn on nine national reports: Britain, Greece, Italy, Netherlands, Portugal, Romania, Russia, Spain and Turkey. The Turkish and Romanian reports were particularly helpful to us in writing Chapter 1 of this book.

Appendix 2   Cases of Child Labour in British Newspapers

The following headlines have appeared during the past 10 years over articles in which specific cases of child labour in Britain are mentioned or described. We have not included articles which refer only to cases in other countries, which refer only to the results of British surveys such as our own, or which refer only to policy debates. The listing is not meant to be comprehensive. However, these headlines give an indication of the range and types of cases which come to the attention of journalists.

Most of the headlines are self-explanatory, but we have added details where some clarification seemed necessary.

'Paper weight lifters: no paperboys and girls aren't getting smaller; their bags just keep getting bigger and heavier' (*The Observer*, 18 December 1988).

'Paper tigers on the newsround [GMB trade union recruiting paper deliverers]' (*The Guardian*, 11 August 1989).

'Scandal of the Possil pieman; Early start as pupils sweat it out in the bakery; Parents "who don't object"' (*Evening Times* (Glasgow), 12 February 1990).

'Plight of paper delivery youth [hospitalized with a protruding spinal disc]' (*The Herald*, 3 March 1990).

'Child labour court cases "just the tip of the iceberg"' (*The Observer*, 16 December 1990).

'Dairy operators are worried over – attacks on milk boys [robbed]' (*East Kilbride News*, 6 March 1991).

'Hardy breed happy to face the sack [of newspapers]' (*The Guardian*, 8 March 1991).

'Child slave anger: long hours, poor pay … and illegal' (*Evening News* (Edinburgh), 9 March 1991).

'In the soup: we expose a factory's illegal child labour that finishes up here [soup can]' (*The People*, 10 March 1991).

'Child labour: can the law deliver?' (*Times Educational Supplement Scotland*, 21 June 1991).

'Jungle kids in circus fury: "werewolfs" act slammed by NSPCC' (*Scottish Sport*, 21 June 1991).

'The blessing and the curse of the studying classes' (*Independent on Sunday*, 7 July 1991).

'Children who break all the rules' (*The Scotsman*, 18 July 1991).

'Campaign to stop the legal exploitation of young workers' (*The Herald*, 29 August 1992).

'Child at work are "open to exploitation"' (*The Herald*, 22 February 1992).

'Illegal child labour ignored, says report' (*The Scotsman*, 22 February 1992).

'Little earners' (*The Guardian*, 3 March 1993).

'Young flower sellers at risk' (*Independent on Sunday*, 27 June 1993).

'Bottom of the working class' (*The Scotsman*, 22 July 1993).

'Girls and boys come out to work' (*Independent on Sunday*, 31 October 1993).

'MP denounces "lenient" fine for child labour man' (*The Scotsman*, 12 November 1993).

'Working for £1 an hour; firm breaks the law with youngsters; Ross High pupil worked with electricity' (*Evening News* (Edinburgh), 12 November 1993).

'"Slave" kids are unfit for school' (*The Glaswegian*, 27 January 1994).

'Jobs for the boys and girls' (*The Big Issue*, 18 February 1994).

'Under age and underpaid' (*The Guardian*, 3 March 1994).

'Schoolchildren who work outside the law: paper-boy, 14, robbed of bike' (*The Journal* (Newcastle-Upon-Tyne), 10 March 1994).

'Child labour laws flouted: bid to protect slave wage youngsters [boy aged eight working late at night in Tyneside fish factory]' (*The Chronicle* (Newcastle-Upon-Tyne), 11 March 1994).

'Big names and big ideas and big big debts [children employed delivering advertising leaflets]' (*Sunday Mail*, 3 April 1884).

'Child "sweat shop" probe: inquiry as youngsters are found in factory: battle to track guilty bosses' (*Lancashire Evening Post*, 12 April 1994).

'Child workers found packing fake-brand jeans in police raid' (*The Guardian*, 13 April 1994).

'Old laws and new work put children at risk: "Snide jeans" raid could not stop under-age workers' (*The Guardian*, 16 April 1994).

'Child labour is the cheapest of all' (*The Observer*, 15 May 1994).

'Victim "too young to work" [15-year-old falls into vat at factory and dies]' (*Express and Star*, 18 June 1994).

'Children "working illegally" on farms' (*The Scotsman*, 22 June 1994).

'On yer bike, boys [newsagent sacks striking paper boys]' (*Daily Record*, 23 August 1994).

'Illegal child labour "beating council controls"' (*The Guardian*, 29 August 1994).

'Please sir, I want to be a prostitute' (*The Guardian*, 29 August 1994).

'Slave boys, scandal that shames Britain; flintstone kids earn £1 a day for paving the streets of London' (*Daily Star*, 19 October 1994).

'Milkboy hurt in fall from float' (*The Herald*, 24 October 1994).

'Street con gangs turn to children: city "Fagans" shock trading standards chiefs' (*Evening Times* (Glasgow), 28 October 1994).

'Market forces: why children work' (*Times Educational Supplement Scotland*, 11 November 1994).

APPENDIX 2   CASES OF CHILD LABOUR IN BRITISH NEWSPAPERS

'Paper-boy robbed' (*East Kilbride News*, 2 December 1994).

'Child labour firm fined £16,500 [paper and packaging factory]' (*The Guardian*, 17 March 1995).

'Boy, 15, died working in factory [breathed solvent fumes and fell into vat]' *(The Guardian*, 29 March 1995).

'Factory boss fined £1,200 after unguarded machine injures boy' (*The Guardian*, 25 April 1995).

'A McJob for every 14-year-old?' (*The Independent*, 29 July 1995).

'It's better than studying, and it isn't a crime [squeegee merchants]' (*The Guardian*, 6 September 1995).

'Paper-round pupils "do better at school": morning work delivers Jack to class bright and early' (*The Times*, 11 September 1995).

'In-care child prostitution revelations suppressed: city council killed findings into how girls contracted sexual diseases' (*The Observer*, 15 October 1995).

'Church wants law eased to help child prostitutes' (*The Guardian*, 18 October 1995).

'Read all about it – press gang scores top marks! [15-year-old with paper round reckons early morning fresh air keeps him alert all day]' (*Daily Telegraph*, 11 November 1995).

'Children worked 12-hour shifts [managing director of bread-making factory fined]' (*The Herald*, 2 December 1995).

'Fine for lorry driver who killed papergirl [knocked off bicycle]' (*The Herald*, 23 January 1996).

'Kittens on the catwalk: after a week in which a 12-year-old girl's modelling career was put on hold, Eleanor Mills finds that the concerns of psychologists and experts cut little ice in the profession' (*The Observer*, 12 May 1996).

'Do you want to be a 12-year-old supermodel? Would any child these days turn down the chance to be fashionable and famous?' (*Independent on Sunday*, 12 May 1996).

'Hard-sell bosses hound poor Pauline, 15, after she tries to kill herself [company demands back payments on hawking contract]' (*Sunday Mail*, 23 June 1996).

'Children "working in Dickensian conditions"' (*The Herald*, 4 July 1996).

'Guard duty: night shift on the site for boys, 13' (*Sunday Mail*, 21 July 1996).

'Bad news over work permits' (*Renfrew and Erskine Gazette*, 8 August 1996).

'Cutthroat traders hire children on the cheap' (*The Observer*, 11 August 1996).

'Sold for sex. Age 15' (*The Guardian*, 21 August 1996).

'Child labour in the High Street' (*Walthamstow Guardian*, 12 September 1996).

'Fine for woman who lured child workers with dance class' (*The Times*, 17 September 1996).

'Firm fined £14,000 for hiring children' (*The Herald*, 17 September 1996).

'Company employed children aged 10–13 in food factory' (*The Guardian*, 17 September 1996).

'Dirt cheap way to sell out childhood: the true scandal of child labour is that we seem unwilling to prevent it' (*The Herald*, 13 December 1996).

'Child labour concern: government deregulation plans will allow 15-year-olds to work 6 hours on Sundays' (*Times Educational Supplement*, 20 December 1996).

'The return of Dickens children' (*The Big Issue in Scotland*, 9 January 1996).

'Work takes toll on children's health and learning, says union' (*Times Educational Supplement Scotland*, 17 January 1997).

'Blast killed security youth: teenager who refused to attend school died on first day at work' (*The Herald*, 18 February 19967).

'Sheriff's concern over boy's death [see previous item]' (*The Herald*, 20 February 1997).

'Model youths dressed to thrill: designer accused of pandering to paedophiles for using school girls at fashion show' (*The Herald*, 22 February 1997).

'Westwood puts 13-year-olds on to catwalk' (*The Guardian*, 22 February 1997).

'Kid skipped school to work a 50-hour week at top hotel: the *Mail* investigates an under-age workers' scandal' (*Sunday Mail*, 6 April 1997).

Appendix 3 Standard Grade Performance and Work Status

Pupils in the Urban and Rural Scotland study of the relationship between work and education (see Chapter 5) were placed in five categories: current workers (low, moderate and high hours), former workers and never worked. These groups were compared for their Standard Grade performance in each subject. Chi square analysis found no significant results.

Subject	n	c^2	
Accounting‡	62	28.0	ns
Accounting and Finance	29	18.8	ns
Art and Design	238	16.5	ns
Biology	237	28.5	ns
Chemistry	305	35.0	ns
Computing Studies	219	47.3	ns
Contemporary Social Studies	21	7.2	ns
Craft and Design	126	22.3	ns
Drama	16	28.0	ns
English	602	33.7	ns
French	384	36.4	ns
Geography	269	27.4	ns
German	171	45.8	ns
Graphic Communication	29	13.7	ns
History	316	37.7	ns
Home Economics	90	18.8	ns
Latin	20	16.1	ns
Mathematics	601	57.6	ns
Modern Studies	161	38.0	ns
Music	114	30.5	ns
Office and Information Studies	206	16.2	ns
Physical Education	150	12.7	ns
Physics	263	20.7	ns
Religious Studies	30	13.1	ns
Science	155	31.5	ns
Social and Vocational Skills	74	20.4	ns
Spanish	31	16.9	ns
Technological Studies	113	18.8	ns
Technical Drawing‡	31 2	5.5	ns

‡ Ordinary Grade subjects.
ns p value not significant.

REFERENCES

Anonymous (1951, first published 1850) *Chapters in the Life of a Dundee Factory Boy*. Dundee: John Scott.
Aronson, P. J., Mortimer, J. T., Zierman, C. and Hacker, M. (1996) Generational differences in family work experiences and evaluations. *Adolescence*, **15**, pp. 25–62.
Bachman, J. G. (1983) Premature affluence: Do high school students earn too much? *Economic Outlook*, **10**, pp. 64–67.
Bachman, J. G. and Schulenberg, J. (1993) How part-time work intensity relates to drug use, problem behaviour, time use and satisfaction among high school seniors: Are these consequences or merely correlates? *Developmental Psychology*, **29**, pp. 220–35.
Balding, J. (1991) A study of working children in 1990. *Education and Health*, **9**, pp. 4–6.
Balding, J. (1993) *Young people in 1992*. Exeter: Schools Health Education Unit, School of Education, University of Exeter.
Balding, J. (1994) *Young people in 1993*. Exeter: Schools Health Education Unit, School of Education, University of Exeter.
Boyd, R. (1994) Child labour within the globalizing economy. *Labour, Capital and Society*, **27**, pp. 153–61.
Bronfenbrenner, U. (1986) Ecology of the family as a context for human development: Research perspectives. *Developmental Psychology*, **41**, pp. 723–42.
Brown, P. (1987) *Schooling ordinary kids: Inequality, unemployment and the new vocationalism*. London: Tavistock.
Call, K. T. (1996) Adolescent work as an 'Area of Comfort' under conditions of family discomfort, in J. T. Mortimer and M. D. Finch (eds) *Adolescents, work and family: An Intergenerational developmental analysis*. Thousand Oaks CA: Sage.
Callender, C. and Kempson, E. (1996) *Student finances: Income, expenditure and take-up of student loans*. London: PSI Publishing.
Cameron, D., Bishop, C. and Sibert, J. R. (1992, 4 July) Farm accidents in children. *British Medical Journal*, **305**, pp. 23–25.
Carvel, J. (1994, 23 June) Britain watches as EU 11 act on workers' rights. *The Guardian*.
Carvel, J. (1995, 20 July) Shephard denies bored pupils will be sent to work. *The Guardian*.
Caulton, T. J. (ed.) (1985) *Children of the Industrial Revolution in Sheffield*. Sheffield: Department of Continuing Education, University of Sheffield.
Central Statistical Office (1994) *Social focus on children*. London: HMSO.
Coffield, F., Borrill, C. and Marshall, S. (1986) *Growing up at the margins*. Milton Keynes: Open University Press.
Cole, S. (1980, July) Send our children to work? *Psychology Today*, pp. 44–67.
Coleman, J. C. (1992) Current views of the adolescent process. In J. C. Coleman (ed.) *The school years: Current issues in the socialisation of young people*, pp. 1–23. New York: Routledge.
Coleman, J. C. and Hendry, L. (1990) *The nature of adolescence*. New York: Routledge.
Combes, A. (1987, 4 December) Not so nice little earners. *Times Educational Supplement*, p. 22.

Courtenay, G. and McAleese, I. (1993) *England and Wales youth cohort study, cohort 5: Aged 16–17 in 1991, Report on Sweep 1*. London: Department for Employment.

Cunningham, H. (1991) *The children of the poor: Representations of childhood since the seventeenth century*. Oxford: Blackwell.

D'Amico, R. (1984) Does employment during high school impair academic progress? *Sociology of Education*, **57**, pp. 152–64.

Davies, E. (1972, 10 November) Work out of school. *Education*, pp. i–iv.

Department of Employment (1993) *People, jobs and progress*. London: Department of Employment.

Eccles, J. S., Midgley, C., Wigfield, A., Buchanan, C. M., Reuman, D., Flanagan, C. and MacIver, D. (1993) Development during adolescence: The impact of stage-environment fit on young adolescents' experiences in schools and in families. *American Psychologist*, **48**, pp. 90–101.

Erikson, E. H. (1968) *Identity: Youth and crisis*. New York: Norton.

Feinstein, C. (1997) Understanding the nature of child work, Paper presented at Conference on Urban Childhood, Trondheim, Norway, 9–12 June.

Finch, M. D., and Mortimer, J. T. (1985) Adolescent work hours and the process of achievement. *Research in the Sociology of Education*, **5**, pp. 171–96.

Finch, M. D., Shanahan, M. J., Mortimer, J. T. and Ryu, S. (1991) Work experience and control orientation in adolescence. *American Sociological Review*, **56**, pp. 597–611.

Finn, D. (1984) Leaving school and growing up: Work experience in the juvenile labour market. In I. E. A. Bates (ed.) *Schooling for the dole? The New Vocationalism*, pp. 17–64. London: Macmillan.

Frow, E. and Frow, R. (1970) *The half-time system in education*. Manchester: Moxton.

Fyfe, A. (1989) *Child labour*. Cambridge: Polity Press.

GMB (1995) *Part-time work among school pupils and college students under age 19*. London: GMB.

Goodnow, J. J. (1988) Children's household work: Its nature and function. *Psychological Bulletin*, **103**, pp. 5–26.

Gray, J. and Jesson, D. (1990) Truancy in secondary schools amongst fifth-year pupils. *Links*, **15**, pp. 25–33.

Greenberger, E. (1983) A researcher in the policy arena: The case of child labor. *American Psychologist*, **38**, pp. 104–10.

Greenberger, E. (1988) Working in teenage America. In J. T. Mortimer and K. M. Borman (eds) *Work experience and psychological development through the life span*. Boulder: Westview Press.

Greenberger, E. and Steinberg, L. (1986) *When teenagers work: The psychological and social costs of adolescent employment*. New York: Basic Books.

Greenberger, E., Steinberg, L. D., Vaux, A. and McAuliffe, S. (1980) Adolescents who work: Effects of part-time employment on family and peer relations. *Journal of Youth and Adolescence*, **9**, pp. 189–202.

Green, D. L. (1990) High School student employment in social context: Adolescents' perceptions of the role of part-time work, *Adolescence*, **25**, pp. 425–34.

Greene, D. and Lepper, M. R. (1974, September) How to turn play into work. *Psychology Today*, pp. 49–54.

Head, J. (1988, 26 February) Children's hours. *New Society*, pp. 20–21.

Health and Safety Commision (1996) *Health and safety statistics, 1994–95*. London: Health and Safety Executive.

Heaven, P. C. L. (1994) *Contemporary adolescence: A social psychological approach*. South Melbourne: Macmillan Education.

Hibbett, A. and Beatson, M. (1995) Young people at work. *Employment Gazette*, **103**, pp. 169–77.

Hobbs, S., Lindsay, S. and McKechnie, J. (1993a) Part-time employment and schooling. *Scottish Educational Review*, **25**, pp. 53–60.

Hobbs, S., Lindsay, S. and McKechnie, J. (1993b) *Children at work: Part-time employment in North Tyneside: A report to North Tyneside Council*. Paisley: University of Paisley.

Hobbs, S., Lindsay, S. and McKechnie, J. (1996a) The extent of child employment in Britain. *British Journal of Education and Work*, **9**, pp. 5–18.

Hobbs, S., McKechnie, J., Lindsay, S. and Stack, N. (1996b) *An evaluation of educational intervention strategies on work permit and knowledge levels*. Paisley: University of Paisley. Unpublished report.

Holmes, M. and Croll, P. (1989) Time spent on homework and academic achievement. *Educational Research*, **31**, pp. 36–45.

House of Commons Employment Committee. (1991) *Child labour: Minutes of evidence*. London: HMSO.

House of Commons European Standing Committee B. (1993) *Protection of young people at work*. London: HMSO.

House of Lords Select Committee on the European Communities (1993) *Protection of young people at work*. London: HMSO.

Howieson, C. (1990) Beyond the gate: Work experience and part-time work among secondary-school pupils in Scotland. *British Journal of Education and Work*, **3**, pp. 49–61.

Hutson, S. (1990) *Saturday jobs: Young people in full-time education working part-time in the city centre*. Swansea, Department of Sociology and Anthropology, University College of Swansea.

Hutt, W. H. (1954) The factory system of the early nineteenth century. In F. A. Hayek (ed.), *Capitalism and the historians,* pp. 156–84. Chicago: University of Chicago Press.

International Labour Organization (1996) *Child labour: Targeting the intolerable*. Geneva: International Labour Office.

Iso-Ahola, S. E. (1980) *The social psychology of leisure and recreation*. Dubuque: Wm C. Brown.

Jesson, J. (1993) Understanding adolescent female prostitution: A literature review. *British Journal of Social Work*, **23**, pp. 517–30.

Johnson, V., Hill, J. and Ivan-Smith, E. (1995) *Listening to smaller voices: Children in an environment of change*. London: ActionAid.

Jolliffe, F., Patel, S., Sparks, Y. and Reardon, K. (1995) *Child employment in Greenwich*. London: Borough of Greenwich, Education Social Work Service.

Jones, G. S. (1976) *Outcast London: A study of the relationship between classes in Victorian society*. Harmondsworth: Penguin.

Labour Research Department (1997, February) Britain's child labour scandal, *Labour Research*, pp. 17–18.

Lavalette, M. (1994) *Child employment in the capitalist labour market*. Aldershot: Avebury.

Lavalette, M. (1996) Thatcher's working children: Contemporary issues of child labour. In J. Pilcher and S. Wagg (eds) *Thatcher's children*, pp. 172–200. London: Falmer Press.

Lavalette, M., McKechnie, J. and Hobbs, S. (1991) *The forgotten workforce: Scottish children at work*. Glasgow: Scottish Low Pay Unit.

Lavalette, M., Hobbs, S., Lindsay, S. and McKechnie, J. (1995) Child employment in Britian: Policy, myth and reality. *Youth and Policy*, pp. 1–15.

Lavalette, M., Lindsay, S., Hobbs, S. and McKechnie, J. (1996) *Child employment in Blackburn*. Liverpool: Child Labour Study Group, Universities of Liverpool and Paisley.

Lee, M. and O'Brien, R. (1995) *The game's up: Redefining child prostitution*. London: Children's Society.

Lepper, M. R. and Greene, D. (1975) Turning play into work: Effects of adult surveillance and extrinsic rewards on children's intrinsic motivation, *Journal of Personality and Social Psychology*, **31**, pp. 479–86.

McKechnie, J., Hobbs, S. and Lindsay, S. Part-time employment and school: A comparison of the work habits at 3rd, 5th and 6th year students, Unpublished paper.

McKechnie, J., Lindsay, S. and Hobbs, S. (1993) *Child employment in Cumbria: A report to Cumbria County Council*. Paisley: University of Paisley.

McKechnie, J., Lindsay, S., and Hobbs, S. (1994) *Still Forgotten: Child Employment in Dumfries and Galloway*. Glasgow: Scottish Low Pay Unit.

McKechnie, J., Lindsay, S., Hobbs, S. and Lavalette, M. (1996) Adolescents' perceptions of the role of part-time work. *Adolescence*, **31**, pp. 193–204.

McLaughlin, C. (1993, 13 October) EC row at British stance on labour laws. *The Scotsman*.

MacLennan, E. (1982) *Child labour in London*. London: Low Pay Unit.

MacLennan, E., Fitz, J. and Sullivan, J. (1985) *Working Children*. London: Low Pay Unit.

Main, B. G. and Raffe, D. (1983) Determinants of employment and unemployment among school leavers: Evidence from the 1979 survey of Scottish school leavers. *Scottish Journal of Political Economy*, **30**, pp. 1–17.

Manning, W. D. (1990) Parenting employed teenagers. *Youth and Society*, **22**, pp. 184–200.

Marsh, H. W. (1991) Employment during high school: Character building or a subversion of academic goals? *Sociology of Education*, **64**, pp. 172–89.

Ministry of Education (1959) *A report of the Central Advisory Council for Education [Crowther Report]*. London: HMSO.

Ministry of Education (1963) *Half our future: A report of the Central Advisory Council for Education [Newsom Report]*. London: HMSO.

Mizen, P. (1992) Learning the hard way: The extent and significance of child working in Britain. *British Journal of Education and Work*, **5**, pp. 5–17.

Morrow, V. (1989) *From 'learners' to 'earners': The development of legislative policies relating to the employment of children and young people in England and Wales, 1900–1969*. Unpublished PhD dissertation, University of Cambridge.

Mortimer, J. T. and Finch, M.D. (1986) The effects of part-time work on self concept and achievement. In K. Borman and J. Reisman (eds) *Becoming a Worker*, pp. 66–89. Norwood, New Jersey: Ablex.

Mortimer, J. T. and Shanahan, M. J. (1994) Adolescent work experience and family relationships. *Work and Occupations*, **21**, pp. 369–84.

Mortimer, J. T. and Finch, M. D. (1996) *Adolescents work and family: An intergenerational developmental analysis*. Thousand Oaks, California: Sage.

Mortimer, J. T., Finch, M., Shanahan, M. and Ryu, S. (1992) Work experience, mental health and behavioural adjustment in adolescence. *Journal of Research on Adolescence*, **2**, pp. 25–57.

Mortimer, J. T., Finch, M. D., Dennehey, K., Lee, C. and Beebe, T. (1994) Work experience in adolescence. *Journal of Vocational Education*, **19**, pp. 39–70.

Mortimer, J. T., Finch, M. D., Ryu, S., Shanahan, M. J. and Call, K. T. (1996) The effects of work intensity on adolescent mental health, achievement and behavioral adjustment: New evidence from a prospective study. *Child Development*, **67**, pp. 1243–61.

Murray, J. (1991) The working children project. In M. Lavalette, J. McKechnie, and S. Hobbs (eds) *The forgotten workforce: Scottish children at work*, pp. 76–95. Glasgow: Scottish Low Pay Unit.

Newman, F. and Holzman, L. (1993) *Lev Vygotsky Revolutionary Scientist*. London: Routledge.

Noller, P. and Callan, V. (1991) *The adolescent in the family*. New York: Routledge.

Notarangelo, R. and Dutter, B. (1991, 9 March). Child slave anger. *Evening News*, pp. 1, 8–9.

Phillips, S. and Sandstrom, K. L. (1990) Parental attitudes toward youth work. *Youth and Society*, **23**, pp. 160–83.

Pond, C. and Searle, A. (1991) *The hidden army: Children at work in the 1990s*. London: Low Pay Unit.

Reddy, N. (1996) Iqbal and the kiss of Judas. *IWGCL Newsletter*, **1**, pp. 15–16.

Renfrew District Council Environmental Services Department (1995) *The manual handling operations regulations 1992 and child employment in Renfrew district*. Renfrew: Renfrew District Council.

Roberts, K., Dench, S. and Richardson, D. (1986) *The changing structure of youth labour markets*. London: Department of Employment.

Saxe, G. (1988) The mathematics of child street vendors. *Child Development*, **59**, pp. 1415–25.

Scruton, R. (1990, 11 February) Why state education is bad for children. *Sunday Telegraph*.
Shanahan, M. J., Elder, G. H., Burchinal, M. and Conger, R. D. (1996) Adolescent earnings and relationships with parents: The work-family nexus in urban and rural ecologies. *Additio*, **15**, pp. 97–128.
Shanahan, M. J., Finch, M., Mortimer, J. T. and Ryu, S. (1991) Adolescent work experience and depressive affect. *Social Psychology Quarterly*, **54**, pp. 299–317.
Sherman, A. (1996, 12 March) Why raising the school leaving age was wrong. *The Guardian*.
Simon, B. (1965) *Education and the labour movement*. London: Lawrence and Wishart.
Sinclair, K. (1996, 13 May) How children work illegally in Scotland. *The Herald*.
Spittles, B. (1973, 8 March) Children at work. *New Society*, pp. 520–21.
Steinberg, L. and Dornbusch, S. M. (1991) Negative correlates of part-time employment during adolescence: Replication and elaboration. *Developmental Psychology*, **27**, pp. 304–13.
Steinberg, L. D., Greenberger, E., Jacobi, M. and Garduque, L. (1981a) Early work experience: A partial antidote for adolescent egocentrism. *Journal of Youth and Adolescence*, **10**, pp. 141–57.
Steinberg, L. D., Greenberger, E., Vaux, A. and Ruggiero, M. (1981b) Early work experience: Effects on adolescent occupational socialization. *Youth and Society*, **12**, pp. 403–22.
Steinberg, L. D., Greenberger, E., Garduque, L., Ruggiero, M. and Vaux, A. (1982a) Effects of working on adolescent development. *Developmental Psychology*, **18**, pp. 385–95.
Steinberg, L. D., Greenberger, E. and Ruggiero, M. (1982b) Assessing job characteristics: When 'perceived' and 'objective' measures don't converge. *Psychological Reports*, **50**, pp. 771–80.
Steinberg, L., Fegley, S. and Dornbusch, S. M. (1993) Negative impact of part-time work on adolescent adjustment: Evidence from a longitudinal study. *Developmental Psychology*, **29**, pp. 171–80.
Stern, D., Stone, J. R., III, Hopkins, C. and McMillion, M. (1990) Quality of students' work experience and orientation toward work. *Youth and Society*, **22**, pp. 263–82.
Stevens, C. J., Putchell, L. A., Ryu, S. and Mortimer, J. T. (1992) Adolescent work and boys' and girls' orientations to the future. *Sociological Quarterly*, **33**, pp. 153–69.
Sylva, K. and Lunt, I. (1985) *Child development: A first course*. Oxford: Blackwell.
Thompson, E. P. (1968, first edition 1961) *The making of the English working class*, 2nd edn. Harmondsworth: Penguin.
Trades Union Congress (1997) *Working classes: A TUC report on school age labour in England and Wales*. London: Trades Union Congress.
Tymms, P. B. and Fitz-Gibbon, C. T. (1992) The relationship between part-time employment and A-level results. *Educational Research*, **34**, pp. 193–99.
Vaughn, S., Schumm, J. S. and Sinagub, J. (1996) *Focus group interviews in education and psychology*. Thousand Oak, California: Sage.
Wallace, C. (1987) *For richer or poorer: Growing up in and out of work*. London: Tavistock.

INDEX

'Aberford' school 80–82
Academic performance *see* GCSE, Standard Grades
Accidents *see* Safety
ActionAid 133
Adolescence 111–115
Africa 119, 133
Afro-Carribean ethnic origin 128–129
Age, changing work 76–78, 117, 132
Age, starting work 73–74
Alcohol consumption 106–108
'Alfredo', child worker, Portugal 8, 12–14, 15, 20
Allerdale, Cumbria 62
'Ana', child worker, Brazil 11, 12–14, 20
'Anne', school student, Cumbria 67, 69
Aronson, P. J. 101
Asia 119, 133
Asian ethnic origin 129
Atlanta, Georgia, USA 10
Aurolac 9
Autonomy, sense of 100–102

Babysitting 41–44
Bachman, J. G. 98, 102, 108–109, 113
Bahia, Brazil 11
Bakery work 142, 144
Balding, J. 26, 29–34, 43–44, 45–46, 49, 50, 54, 57, 130
Bangladeshi ethnic origin 129
Barrow-in-Furness, Cumbria 62–78
'Bartown' school 80–82
BBC TV 140
Beatson, M. 24, 29–34, 37–38, 41, 42, 43–45, 128
Bedford 45
Behavioural effects of employment 106–108
Berthon, S. 140
Big Issue, The, magazine 143
Big Issue in Scotland, The, magazine 145
Birmingham 22, 44
Bishop, C. 42
Blackburn 2, 39–61, 120, 129–131
Blair, Tony, MP 21
Board of Education 19–20

Bonded Labour Liberation Front, Pakistan 7–8
'Bonnie', child worker, United States 10–11, 12–14
Boyd, R. 52
Brazil 11, 99
British Journal of Education and Work 4
Bronfenbrenner, U. 113–114, 121
Brown, P. 30–34
Bucharest, Romania 9
Building sites 144, 145
Burkina Faso 1

California, USA 12, 97
Call, K. T. 103, 104
Callaghan, James, MP 21
Callan, V. 102
Callender, C. 117
Cameron, D. 42, 60
Carribean ethnic origin 128
Carlisle 62–78
Carpet Manufacturers Association, Lahore 8
Carpet weaving 7–8, 11
Carvel, J. 22, 23, 122
Case Histories
   Cumbria 65–69
   International 7–14
Caulton, T. J. 18
Central Statistical Office 37
Channel 4 TV 140
Chapters in the Life of a Dundee Factory Boy 16
Chaudhary, D. 140
Child, definition 1–2
Child beauty contests 10–11, 140
Child labour, definition 1–3, 31, 129
Child labour, extent, Britain 24–38, 128
Child labour, extent, global 7
Child Poverty Action Group 117
Child Slaves, TV programme 140
Child soldiers 12
Children and Young Persons Act, 1933 19, 25, 46, 55, 96, 123
Children and Young Persons (Scotland) Act, 1937 20, 46, 55, 96, 123
Children in Chains, TV programme 140
Children of the Loom, TV programme 140

INDEX

Chimney Sweep Act, 1875 17
Chronicle, The, newspaper, Newcastle-Upon-Tyne 143
Cigarette smoking 106–108
Circus performing 142
Clwyd, Ann, MP 122
Clydeside 44
Coffield, F. 112
Colchester, Essex 15
Cole, S. 100–102, 112
Coleman, J. C. 112
Combes, A. 30–34
Commitment to education 82–88
Conservative Party 22, 23
Consumer goods 13, 21
Convention on the Rights of the Child vii, 6, 98, 127–128
Copeland, Cumbria 62–78
Cost and benefits 96–115, 137–138
Courtenay, G. 29–34
Coventry 44
Croll, P. 30–34
Crowther Report 20
Cumbria 1, 3, 39–61, 62–78, 88–91, 93–94, 120
  County Council 2, 62–63
Cunningham, H. 17

Daily Record, newspaper 143
Daily Star, newspaper 143
Daily Telegraph, newspaper 144
D'Amico, R. 108
'David', child worker, Wales 8–9, 12–14, 20
Davies, E. 20, 25–29, 54, 79–80, 82
Defoe, D. 15
Delinquency 108–108
Delivery work 41–44, 142, 143, 144
Department of Education and Employment 22
Department of Employment 24, 30, 37
Department of Health 23, 119, 122–123, 125
Department of Health and Social Security 25, 79
Dispatches, TV series 140
Dornbusch, S. M. 98, 101, 102, 106, 107, 108
Drug consumption 9, 106–108
Dubois, H. 140
Dumfries and Galloway 2, 39–61, 120, 125
Dundee 16
Dutter, B. 30–34

Earnings 47–50, 73
East Kilbride News, newspaper 142, 144
Eccles, J. S. 112
Ecological model of adolescence 113–115
Eden, Cumbria 62
Education Act, 1880 18
Education Act, 1918 18
Education Act, 1936 19
Education Act, 1944 20, 25
Education, and child labour 14, 21–22, 79–95, 145
Egypt 10
'Elaine', school student, Cumbria 67, 69

Elementary Education Act, 1870 18
Employment of Children Act, 1903 19
Employment of Children Act, 1973 20
Employment of Women, Young Persons and Children Act, 1921 19
England 2, 15, 22, 29, 31, 34–36, 39, 62, 128
Erikson, E. H. 100, 112
'Errol', child worker, Turkey 9–10, 12–14
Ethnicity 128–129
Europe ix
Europe, Eastern 119
Europe, Western 121
European Parliament 23
European Union 22, 118
Evening News, newspaper, Edinburgh 142, 143
Evening Times, newspaper, Glasgow, 142, 143
Exploitation 143
Express and Star, newspaper 143

Factory Act, 1833 17
Factory Act, 1844 17
Factory Act, 1874 18
Factory work 142, 143, 144
Family life and employment 13, 101–104, 130
Farm work 12, 41–44, 143
'Fatima', child worker, Egypt 10, 12–14, 20
Feinstein, C. 136–137
Finch, M. D. 100, 104, 105, 108, 111, 113, 130, 137
Finn, D. 30–34, 54
Fitz-Gibbon, C. T. 28
Flower selling 143
Forsyth, Michael, MP 24
Frow, E. 18
Frow, R. 18
Future employment 104–106, 118
Fyfe, A. 121

Garlic picking 12
GCSE performance 88–91
Gender differences 50–55, 75–76, 100, 106, 128
General Election, 1997 123
General National Vocational Qualifications 22
'George', school student, Cumbria 65, 69
Georgia, USA 10
Glasgow 1
Glaswegian, The, newspaper 143
GMB trade union 22, 116
Goodnow, J. J. 50, 129
Granada TV 140
Gray, J. 83
Great Britain, child employment passim
Greece 141
Green, D.L. 94, 134
Greenberger, E. 44, 50, 94, 97, 98, 99, 100, 102, 103, 104–105, 106, 107–108, 110, 113, 114, 123, 137
Greene, D. 6
Greenwich 44, 125, 128
Guardian, The, newspaper 1, 22, 142, 143, 144, 145

INDEX

Half-time Working 17–18
Hawking 41–44, 144
Head, J. 49
Headlines, newspapers 1, 22, 119, 142–145
Health and safety 58–61, 142, 143, 144, 145
Health and Safety Act, 1974 74–75
Health and Safety Executive 59–60
Health and Safety Commission 59–60
Heaven, P. C. L. 112
Hendry, L. 112
Herald, The, newspaper, Glasgow 142, 143, 144, 145
Hibbett, A. 24, 29–34, 37–38, 41, 42, 43–45, 128
Higher education students 117
Hobbs, S. 4, 34, 43, 82, 126–127
Holmes, M. 30–34
Hotel and catering work 41–44, 145
Hours worked 44–47, 71–73, 62–88, 108–109
House of Commons Employment Committee 122
House of Commons European Standing Committee B 24
House of Lords Select Committee on the European Communities 24
Howieson, C. 29
Hunt, David, MP 22–23
Hutson, S. 15, 28–34
Hutt, W. H. 15

Independent, The, newspaper, 144
Independent on Sunday, The, newspaper 142, 143, 144
India 11, 140
Indian ethnic origin 128–129
Industrial Revolution 14–16
International Bonded Labour Foundation 8
International Labour Organization 1, 6, 7
International Movement for Working Children 133
International Working Group on Child Labour 2, 133, 136, 141
'Ion', child worker, Romania 9, 12–14
Iqbal Masih 7–8, 15
Iso-Ahola, S.E. 6
Italy 141

Jasmine picking 10
'Jason', school student, Cumbria 66, 69
'Jennifer', school student, Cumbria 66–67
Jesson, D. 83
Jesson, J. 131
'Joan', school student, Cumbria 68–69
Job types *see* Types of job
'John', school student, Cumbria 68, 69
Johnson, V. 133
Jolliffe, F. 43–44, 50, 57, 128–129
Jones, G.S. 18
Journal, The, newspaper, Newcastle-Upon-Tyne 143
'Juanito', child worker, United States 12–14

'Karen', school student, Cumbria 67
Kempson, E. 117
Kendall, Cumbria 62
Kentucky 10
Kenya 1

Labour Research Department 22
Lahore 8
Lake District 62
Lancashire Evening Post, newspaper 22, 143
Latin America 119, 133
Lavalette, M. 2, 3, 15, 22, 24, 26, 30–34, 36, 40, 43, 45, 47, 53, 120, 121, 127, 129, 131, 133, 136
Lee, M. 131
Lee-Wright, P. 140
Leeds Mercury, newspaper 16
Legality 55–58, 73–74, 142, 143
Legislation 122–127 *see also* individual Acts
Lepper, M.R. 6
Lindsay, S. 2, 3, 43
Liverpool, University of 2
London 16, 22
Look Who's Working, TV programme 140
'Louise', school student, Cumbria 68–69
Louisville, Kentucky, USA 10
Low Pay Network 22
Low Pay Unit, London 22, 30, 37–38, 117, 122
Luggage porters 8–9
Lunt, I. 102
Luton 45

MacLennan, E. 22, 26, 30–34, 45, 48, 49, 54, 57, 121
Main, B. G. 29–34
Manchester 22
Manchester Low Pay Unit 22, 117
Manning, W. D. 101–103
Marmaris, Turkey 9–10
Marsh, H. W. 97, 99, 112
McAleese, I. 29–34
McKechnie, J. 22, 34, 43, 50, 110, 134
McLaughlin, C. 22
Methodology 2–3, 25–26, 130–139
Mexico 12
Migrant labour 12
Ministry of Education 20
Mizen, P. 30–34, 43–44, 45, 49, 54, 134
Modelling 144, 145
Monks, J. 22
MORI 22
Morrow, V. 19, 20, 135
Mortimer, J. T. 98, 101, 103, 104, 105, 107, 108, 109, 110, 111, 113, 114, 118, 130, 137
Murray, J. 28, 127
Myers, W. E. x

Netherlands 141
New Lanark 17
Newsom Report 20
Nicholson, Emma, MP 122

INDEX

Nigeria ix
Nightshift 144
Nike 1
Nile delta, Egypt 10
Noller, P. 102
North Tyneside 2, 39–61, 120, 125
Notarangelo, R. 30–34
Nuffield Foundation 2

Oastler, R. 16
O'Brien, R. 131
Observer, The, newspaper 142, 143, 144
One World Northern Ireland 117
Owen, R. 17
Oxford English Dictionary 5

Pageant, magazine 10
Painted Babies, TV programme 140
Paisley, University of 2
Pakistan 7
Pakistani ethnic origin 129
'Paul', school student, Cumbria 68, 69
Peers 102–104
People, The, newspaper 142
Personal choice 13
'Peter', school student, Cumbria 66
Phillips, S. 104
Play, definition 6
Pond, C. 22, 24, 29–34, 37–38, 41, 43–44, 47, 48, 52, 58, 59, 101, 129, 130, 131
Portugal 8, 141
Poverty 12–13, 91–120–121
Prostitution 11, 12, 131, 143, 144
Psychosomatic distress 106
Public Eye, TV series 140

Questionnaires 2–3, 27–28, 34, 130–131

Raffe, D. 29–34
Reddy, N. 7
Reebok 1
Reebok Prize 8
Renfrew and Erskine Gazette, newspaper 144
Renfrew District Council Environmental Services Department 125
'Reserve army' hypothesis 120–121
Road laying 143
Roberts, K. 29–34
Romania 9, 141

Safety 58–61, 74–75
Sandstrom, K.L. 104
'Sanji', child worker, India 11, 12–14, 15, 20
Santa Barbara, Feast of 11
Save The Children Fund 117
Saxe, G. 99
School attendance 79, 83–91
School Attendance Officers 18

Schulenberg, J. 98, 108–109, 113
Scobie, E. 140
Scotland 2, 17, 19–20, 29, 31, 34–36, 39, 118, 128, 140
Scotland, rural 82–88 *see also* Dumfries and Galloway
Scotland, Urban 39–61, 82–88
Scotsman, The newspaper 1, 142, 143
Scottish Low Pay Unit 2, 22, 117
Scottish Office 23
Scottish Office Education Department 2
Scottish Reporters, TV series 140
Scottish Sport, newspaper 142
Scottish Television 140
Scruton, R. 21–22, 122
Searle, A. 22, 24, 29–34, 37–38, 41, 43–44, 47, 48, 52, 58, 59, 101, 129, 130, 131
Security work 144, 145
Sellafield, Cumbria 62
Shaftesbury, Lord 14, 17
Shanahan, M. J. 101, 103, 107, 114
Sheffield 18
Shepherd, Gillian, MP 22, 122
Sherman, A. 21–22
Shop work 41–44, 144
Sibert, J. R. 42
Sigworth, M. 140
Simon, B. 18, 19
Sinclair, K. 125
Socialist Parties 23
Somalia vii
South Lakeland, Cumbria 62–78
Southern Charm Pageant 10
Spain 141
Spittles, B. 30–34
Squeegee merchants 144
Standard Grade Examinations 81–88, 146
Steinberg, L.D. 27, 44, 50, 94, 97, 98, 99, 100–101, 102, 103, 104, 105, 106, 107–108, 110, 113, 114, 132, 137
Stern, D. 105, 111
Stevens, C.J. 106, 107
Stonebreaking 8
Street children 9, 99
Stress 106–108
Sunday Mail, newspaper 1, 22, 143, 144, 145
Sylva, K. 102

Taunton, Somerset 15
Television programmes 7, 140
Tennessee 10–11
Thompson, E.P. 15–16
Time To Listen, video 133
Times, The, newspaper 144
Times Educational Supplement, newspaper 145
Times Educational Supplement Scotland, newspaper 142, 143, 144
Tourism 9–10, 11, 21
Trades Union Congress 22, 116–117, 130
Treays, J. 140

INDEX

Truancy *see* School attendance
Turkey 9–10, 141
Turning A Blind Eye, TV programme 140
Tymms, P. B. 28
Types of job 109–110
Tyneside *see* North Tyneside

Undercover Britain, TV series 140
United Nations viii
  Convention on the Rights of the Child, *see separate entry* General Assembly 6
United States of America vii, 2, 12, 94, 98, 99, 109, 118, 119, 121, 123, 140, 141
Universities *see* individual University names

Vaughn, S. 134
Voices of children 133–136
Vygotsky, L.S. 99

Waiting at table 41–44
Wales 8–9, 22, 29, 62, 128
Wallace, C. 30–34
Walthamstow Guardian, newspaper 144
What Price The Born-to-spend Generation? TV programme 140
Whitehaven 62
'William', school student, Cumbria 68
Work, definition 1
Work patterns 93–95
Work permits 55–58, 74, 124, 144
Workington 62
World in Action, TV series 140
World War, First 19
World War, Second 19–20

Yeo, Tim, MP 24
Youth Cohort Study 29

Published by The Stationery Office Limited and available from:

The Stationery Office Bookshops
71 Lothian Road, Edinburgh EH3 9AZ
(counter service only)
59–60 Holborn Viaduct, London EC1A 2FD
(counter service and fax orders only)
Fax 0171-831 1326
68-69 Bull Street, Birmingham B4 6AD
0121-236 9696 Fax 0121-236 9699
33 Wine Street, Bristol BS1 2BQ
0117-926 4306 Fax 0117-929 4515
9-21 Princess Street, Manchester M60 8AS
0161-834 7201 Fax 0161-833 0634
16 Arthur Street, Belfast BT1 4GD
01232 238451 Fax 01232 235401
The Stationery Office Oriel Bookshop
The Friary, Cardiff CF1 4AA
01222 395548 Fax 01222 384347

The Stationery Office publications are also available from:

The Publications Centre
(mail, telephone and fax orders only)
PO Box 276, London SW8 5DT
General enquiries 0171-873 0011
Telephone orders 0171-873 9090
Fax orders 0171-873 8200

Accredited Agents
(see Yellow Pages)

and through good booksellers

Printed in Scotland for The Stationery Office Limited J32494, C10, CC003808 11/97

To Lois, Margaret and Sandra

Children in Society Series
Edited by Stewart Asquith
Centre for the Child & Society
University of Glasgow

Other Titles:
Families and the Future
Supporting Families
The Kilbrandon Report

Child Employment in Britain
A Social and Psychological Analysis